HARPER'S
WORLD OF THE NEW TESTAMENT

To Gail

HARPER'S
World of the
New Testament

Edwin Yamauchi

1817

HARPER & ROW, PUBLISHERS, SAN FRANCISCO
Cambridge, Hagerstown, Philadelphia, New York
London, Mexico City, São Paulo, Sydney

HARPER'S WORLD OF THE NEW TESTAMENT.
Copyright © 1981 by Lion Publishing. All rights
reserved. Printed in Italy. No part of this book
may be used or reproduced in any manner
whatsoever without written permission except in
the case of brief quotations embodied in critical
articles and reviews. For information address
Harper & Row, Publishers, Inc., 10 East 53rd Street,
New York, NY 10022. Published simultaneously in
Canada by Fitzhenry & Whiteside, Limited,
Toronto.

FIRST U.S. EDITION

**Library of Congress Cataloging in Publication
Data**

Yamauchi, Edwin M
  Harper's world of the New Testament.

  1. Bible. N.T.—History of contemporary events.
2. Judaism—History—Greco-Roman period,
332 B.C.–A.D. 210. 3. Rome—Civilization. 4. Rome—
Religion. I. Title. II. Title: World of the New
Testament.
BS2407.Y35 1981   225.9'5   80–8606
ISBN 0–06–069708–3

81 82 83 84 85 10 9 8 7 6 5 4 3 2 1

Editorial and additional material
Ruth Connell
Derek Williams

Illustrations
Evelyn Bartlett: 112, 115, 119, 120, 121
Roger Dicks: 104
David Reddick: 23
Edward Ripley: 49, 55, 85, 88
Ray Wright: 46, 86, 92, 110, 114

Maps
Roy Lawrance
Lesley Passey

Printed in Italy by New Interlitho S.P.A. Milan.

The photographs in this book are reproduced by
permission of the following photographers and
organizations:

Archivio Fotografico del Musea di Roma:
82 (above)
British Museum: 16 (below), 38 (above), 40, 48, 67,
77 (left)
Cabinetto Fotografico Nationale: 109
Camera Press: 3, 10, 16 (above), 22
David Harris: 14 (both), 15 (all)
Sonia Halliday Photographs: F. H. C. Birch 9, 30, 33,
41, 52, 71 (right), 77, 80 (left), 82 (below); Pru Grice
29; Sonia Halliday 1, 5, 7 (right), 18, 20, 28, 35, 37, 38
(below), 45, 47, 50, 57, 65, 69, 71 (left), 80 (right), 81,
95, 102, 106, 107 (both), 112, 116, 118, 122; Jane
Taylor 6, 12, 13, 27, 32, 60
Lion Publishing, David Alexander: 21
Mansell Collection: 4, 8, 31, 39, 44, 49, 51 (both), 54,
56, 61, 66, 72 (both), 74, 75, 78 (left), 89, 91, 96, 100,
101, 108, 113 (below), 121, 123, 124 (all), 125, 126,
128
W. Metz: 7 (below left), 25
Ann and Bury Peerless: 26
Ronald Sheridan: 42, 78 (right), 97, 99, 113 (above)
Stephen Travis: 7 (above), 17

Contents

Preface

The first century AD was a cultural crossroads. The Roman Empire was at its zenith. The legions conquered new lands not only with weapons but also with ideas. They took with them new religions and customs, leaving behind new roads and cities. The foundations of the modern world were being laid.

And in a remote corner of the Empire, foundations of another kind were being laid. Unnoticed by all save a handful of jealous opponents and a motley band of supporters, a new religious movement had begun. Within a century it had spread across the whole of southern Europe and into Africa and Asia. Three hundred years later it was to become the official religion of the Empire.

Christianity had fulfilled, beyond all expectation, the jibe of its early opponents: it had turned the world upside down. Over the centuries, it has become an even more potent, and longer-lasting, agent of change than the Empire that spawned it.

When it began, Christianity was closely tied to the political events of the time. In the Christmas story of the birth of Jesus, there was 'no room at the inn'. The emperor had called for a census requiring families to return to their ancestors' home towns. Thirty years or so later Jesus was crucified under Roman law on the pretext of leading an insurrection against the occupying power. And the first great missionary of Christianity, Paul of Tarsus, used both his knowledge of contemporary literature and his Roman citizenship to good effect in proclaiming his message.

Roman politics was not the only influence on the young faith. Greek culture – the Hellenistic world – was also crucial to it. 'Common' Greek was used throughout the ancient world as the language for commerce, travel and culture. The new cities, with their theatre and market place, fine streets, temples and public buildings, were often the centres of their area and so a natural starting-point for evangelism. Though Jesus and his immediate followers spoke Aramaic, the New Testament was aimed at the whole of the then known world; it was written in Greek. And its contents had to take into account the Greek ways of thinking in which its readers were steeped.

Later, Greek philosophy was to threaten the core of

Christian belief when it was assimilated into the church's theology. But it also provided the catalyst which prompted the church to define its teachings more closely.

So the rise of Christianity cannot be fully understood without reference to its historical and cultural background. The aim of this book is to chart that background. It does not complicate the picture with constant cross-references to the New Testament. These are only mentioned when demanded by the context. It is not the purpose of the book to re-tell the story of Jesus, Paul and their confederates in their cultural environment. Rather, it is concerned with the world of the conquerors and priests, the architects and scholars, the warriors and merchants who make up the backcloth to (and sometimes were affected by) the coming of Jesus and the new church.

The result is both a book that sheds light on the New Testament and an informative introduction to the first century. Its main aim is to show how crucial to our understanding of the New Testament is an appreciation of its setting. The events it records took place in a real world, at an actual time in history, and in places that can still be seen, photographed and appreciated today.

THE JEWISH WORLD

alestine, homeland of the Jews in ancient mes, was a relatively tiny land. It was only 50 miles (240 km) from Dan in the north to eersheba in the south, and less than 50 iles (80 km) from Jaffa in the west to ericho in the east. Its area of less than 0,000 square miles is somewhat smaller an Belgium and a little larger than the ate of Vermont, USA.

Yet Palestine's position, as the corridor for land traffic between Egypt and Syria/Mesopotamia, made it of vital concern to those major powers. The Megiddo Pass, through which the international highway runs, was the scene of countless battles fought to control the route. Between the death of Alexander the Great in 323 BC and the battle of Ipsus in 301 BC Palestine was crossed or occupied seven times by the Egyptian and Syrian armies.

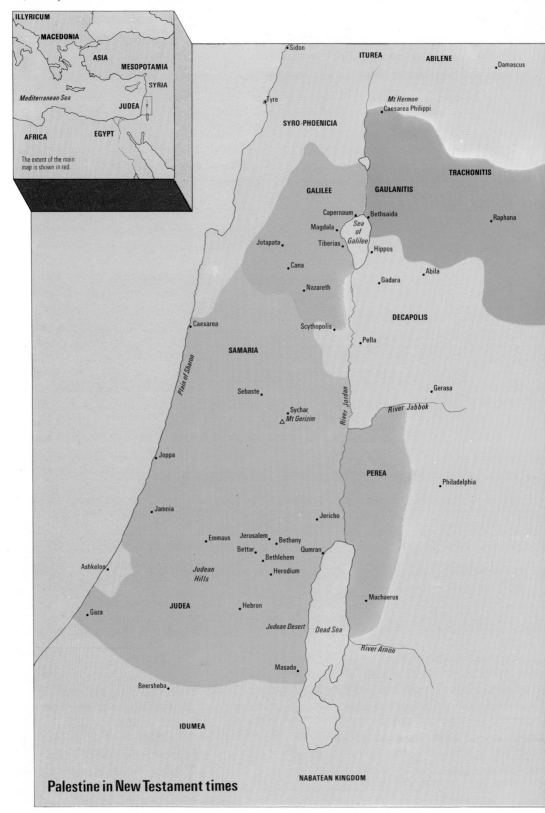

ILLYRICUM

MACEDONIA

ASIA
MESOPOTAMIA

SYRIA

Mediterranean Sea

JUDEA

AFRICA   EGYPT

The extent of the main
map is shown in red.

Sidon

ITUREA   ABILENE
                          Damascus

Tyre   Mt Hermon
            Caesarea Philippi

SYRO-PHOENICIA   TRACHONITIS

GALILEE   GAULANITIS

Capernaum   Bethsaida
                          Raphana
Magdala   Sea
           of
           Galilee
Jotapata   Tiberias   Hippos

Cana   Abila

Nazareth   Gadara

Caesarea   DECAPOLIS

Scythopolis

SAMARIA   Pella

Plain of Sharon

Sebaste   Gerasa

Sychar   River Jabbok
△ Mt Gerizim

River Jordan

Joppa

PEREA
                Philadelphia
Jamnia

Jericho

Emmaus   Jerusalem   Bethany
          Bettar   Qumran
                Bethlehem
Ashkelon   Herodium

Judean
Hills   Machaerus

JUDEA   Hebron

Gaza   Judean Desert   Dead Sea

River Arnon

Masada

Beersheba

IDUMEA

Palestine in New Testament times

NABATEAN KINGDOM

Jews under Roman rule

The Maccabean Revolt

Antiochus: 175–164 BC

The conquests of Alexander the Great led to the spread of the Greek culture and language across a wide area. The generals who succeeded Alexander, Ptolemy in Egypt and Seleucus in Syria, attempted to unite their subjects with policies which combined Greek and native ingredients.

The Seleucid ruler, Antiochus IV Epiphanes, provoked the Jews into a revolt by his radical attempt to promote Greek culture (a process often known as 'hellenization'). He did win the support of the aristocratic Jews, who were keen to be recognized as cultured 'Greeks'. The brother of the Jewish high priest changed his name from Jesus to the Greek Jason, and bribed Antiochus so that he could become the high priest. He scandalized other Jews by building a gymnasium where nude exercises went on within sight of the temple. Jason ended his life in exile in Sparta.

Antiochus forbade the observance of the sabbath and the practice of circumcision, and forced the Jews to eat food they regarded as ceremonially unclean. When a mother and her seven sons refused to defile themselves by eating pork they were martyred. Sacred prostitution associated with the Syrian goddess was practiced in the temple precincts. In December

The Festival of Lights is still celebrated each year in Jewish homes. Lamps with eight burners are lit because, according to tradition, one day's supply of oil for the seven-branched lampstand lasted eight days after the temple had been rededicated in 165 BC.

167 BC, a pig was sacrificed on an altar erected to the Greek god Zeus. This was taken to be 'The Awful Horror' prophesied by Daniel.

Daniel 11 : 31

Jewish opposition was led by a priest called Mattathias and his sons, the oldest of whom was Judas, called Maccabaeus, 'The Hammer'. The Maccabean Revolt succeeded in recapturing the temple in December 165. Jews today celebrate the holiday of Hanukkah, the 'Festival of Lights', to commemorate this event.

After Judas was killed in 161 BC, his brother Jonathan took over leadership. He was also appointed high priest in 153, the first of the long line of Hasmoneans (named after Simon, the last surviving brother of Judas) who were to control that post until 36 BC. This joining of political and religious leadership in the hands of one family was not welcomed by many of the devout Jews.

John Hyrcanus, a nephew of Judas and Jonathan, won political independence for the Jews in 129 BC. This lasted only to 63 BC when the Romans annexed Palestine.

The Roman conquest

Pompey was the Roman general who ended Palestine's political independence.

The Roman leader Pompey was given unlimited powers in 66 BC to clear the Mediterranean of pirates, a task which he efficiently accomplished in three months. Almost as an afterthought he marched into Palestine, where two brothers were squabbling over the high priest's office. He sided with the older brother, Hyrcanus, against the ambitious Aristobulus. In 63 Pompey captured Jerusalem, and had the audacity to enter the Holy of Holies of the temple, which only the Jewish high priest entered once a year. The fact that he touched none of the temple treasures did little to lessen the indignation of the Jews.

Pompey also organized the Decapolis, a league of ten cities which were Greek colonies, and included Scythopolis (Bethshean) south of the Sea of Galilee, and nine others in Syria and Jordan, among them Damascus, Philadelphia (Amman), Pella, Gerasa and Gadara.

The Herods

The Idumaeans were a tribe who had been forced by the Nabataean Arabs westwards into southern Judea, where they had been forcibly converted to Judaism by the Hasmonean rulers of Palestine. The Idumaeans were for this reason Jews of a recent and suspect background. At the same time they were shrewd, and had no scruples about making political deals with the Romans for their own advantage.

Antipater governed them from about 47 BC. He also served as an advisor to Hyrcanus, and gained the confidence of Pompey. When Julius Caesar was besieged in Alexandria in 48 BC it was Antipater who persuaded the Jews to aid Caesar. In gratitude Caesar gave the Jews important privileges.

Antipater's son, Herod the Great, was an opportunist of the

highest order. During the tumultuous years of the Roman civil wars he skilfully shifted his allegiance from Pompey to Caesar to Antony to Octavian (Augustus). Because he was such an able soldier the Romans valued his services. He provided a strong buffer-state for Rome against the Nabataean Arabs to the south and the Parthians to the east.

Herod was appointed king of Judea by the Romans in 40 BC, and was supported by Roman soldiers in his fight to gain control of Judea in 37. From that time he relied on Gentile soldiers, including the Celtic bodyguard of Cleopatra which had been granted to him by Octavian. He transformed the ancient city of Samaria into Sebaste for his foreign mercenaries. He also built Palestine's first deep-water port of Caesarea.

The deep-water port Herod built at Caesarea made the city an important trade centre. Two massive breakwaters once protected an area of about 3½ acres.

Though successful in politics, Herod was bitterly unhappy in his private life. He married ten wives, including the beautiful Hasmonean princess, Mariamne. Though he loved her passionately, he suspected her of infidelity and had her executed. Later, in 7 BC, he had her two sons killed. When he found that his favourite son, Antipater, had been plotting against him, he had him executed – just five days before his own death in 4 BC. It was this paranoid monarch who ordered the massacre of the babies in Bethlehem after the birth of Jesus.

Matthew 2: 13-18

Our system of dating BC/AD was devised by a monk in the

sixth century AD. However, he miscalculated the reign of the Emperor Augustus by four years. Jesus must have been born before Herod's death in 4 BC, a date which has been established by astronomical calculations.

Herod's kingdom was divided between his three sons: Archelaus inherited Judea; Antipas was given Galilee and Perea (Transjordan); Philip inherited largely Gentile areas east of the Sea of Galilee.

4 BC–AD 34

Mark 9:2-8

Mark 8:29

Philip's rule was just and relatively uneventful. It was in Philip's territory that Jesus was transfigured, on the slopes of Mount Hermon. At Caesarea Philippi, at the foot of Hermon, Peter declared that Jesus was the Christ.

Antipas, the tetrarch of Galilee and Perea, was called 'that fox' by Jesus because of his craftiness. He was denounced by John the Baptist for his adulterous relationship with Herodias, the former wife of his half-brother. After a seductive dance by her daughter, probably Salome, Antipas rashly promised her whatever she asked. He reluctantly fulfilled her request by presenting John's head on a dish to Herodias. It was her nagging insistence which proved to be Antipas' undoing. When he asked to be upgraded from tetrarch to king in AD 39, he was instead banished with his wife to France.

Mark 6: 29

Archelaus was 'a chip off his father's block'. As his first official act, he slaughtered 3,000 of his enemies. When Joseph and Mary returned from Egypt, they wisely avoided his territory and settled in Galilee. Archelaus' rule was so oppressive that Jews and Samaritans united in successfully requesting his deposition in AD 6. This paved the way for direct rule by Roman governors.

The division of Herod's kingdom

An aerial view of the Herodium, the fortress built by Herod on a hilltop 7 miles/12 kms south of Jerusalem.

Another important leader, Agrippa I, was a grandson of Herod the Great. He was brought up in Rome in close contact with the imperial family. As a personal friend of the Emperor Caligula he was given first the territories of Philip, then after AD 39 Galilee and Perea. When Caligula was assassinated in 41, Agrippa helped in the selection of Claudius as emperor. As a reward, Agrippa was made king over Judea and Samaria – the first king to rule over the Jews in a generation. To maintain his popularity with his subjects he persecuted the Christians and killed James the son of Zebedee, one of the twelve apostles. He was struck down with a fatal illness in the theatre at Caesarea.

Acts 12: 1
Acts 12: 21-23

His son, Agrippa II, later ruled as king in title, though real power once again rested with the Roman governor. Together with his sister, Drusilla, who was married to the Roman governor Felix, Agrippa II heard the apostle Paul's eloquent defence of his behaviour, recorded in The Acts of the Apostles. Agrippa opposed the Jewish Revolt which broke out in AD 66, since he owed his throne to Rome. Another sister, Berenice, became the mistress of Titus, the Roman general who captured Jerusalem in 70.

Acts 24

Herod's buildings

Herod was a prodigious builder, as recent archaeological excavations have shown. His rebuilding of the temple in Jerusalem, begun in 19 BC, was admired by Jesus' disciples, according to Mark, chapter 13. Final work on the temple was completed just six years before it was destroyed by the Romans in AD 70. All that remains today is the great platform whose western side is the Wailing Wall, where Jews today still lament the destruction of the temple. Spectacular remains have also been uncovered at the fortress of Masada on the western shore and of Machaerus on the eastern shore of the Dead Sea. Machaerus was the fortress where John the Baptist was imprisoned. Other splendid structures from Herod's time have been found at Jericho, where Herod died, and at Herodium, where he was buried.

The Roman occupation

The Romans taxed the Jews heavily. This fourth-century AD relief shows peasants paying their rent.

From AD 6, except for the brief rule of Agrippa I (AD 41–44), until the outbreak of the First Jewish War in 66, a series of fourteen Roman governors ruled Judea.

The governor of Judea, known as a *praefect* or *procurator*, came from the Roman equestrian class, and was subordinate to the legate of Syria at Damascus. Judea was considered a minor province; its governor had at his disposal only a small force of about 3,000 auxiliary soldiers, mostly stationed at Caesarea. On festival occasions, such as the Jewish Passover, a cohort of about 500 soldiers would be stationed in the Fortress Antonia in Jerusalem, overlooking the temple grounds.

Pontius Pilate governed from AD 26 to 36, under the Emperor Tiberius. He was a protégé of the powerful Sejanus, head of the praetorian guard in Rome. Pilate outraged the Jews by several tactless actions. For instance he used temple funds to build an aqueduct, and introduced military standards bearing the emperor's image into Jerusalem, which offended Jewish religious traditions. He met opposition with ruthless force. On the other hand, he yielded to Jewish pressures to

Matthew 27: 15-26

have Jesus crucified as a royal pretender. This occurred either in 30, or as some writers have argued, in 33 after the fall of Sejanus, when Pilate's own position became insecure.

As his name Felix – Latin for 'fortunate' – indicates, the governor of Judea from 52 to 60 was a freedman, or former slave. His brother Pallas was the secretary of the Roman treasury under the Emperor Claudius (41–54). The historian Tacitus says of him: 'With every sort of cruelty and lust he exercised royal functions in the spirit of a slave.' It was his

Acts 24: 26

hope for a bribe which kept the apostle Paul imprisoned in Caesarea.

When Festus (60–62) succeeded Felix as governor, Paul took advantage of his right as a Roman citizen to appeal direct to Caesar, who at that time was Nero.

The Roman occupation through Jewish eyes.

The greatest blow felt by the Jews was to their national pride. They believed that God had chosen them to be his special people. They looked forward to the day when the nations of the world would come to worship God in Jerusalem. Instead, the Romans and their puppet rulers desecrated their holy places, and flouted their laws and customs.

Herod the Great built a temple to Augustus in Caesarea. Inside it were statues of the emperor depicted as Zeus and Rome personified as Hera: statues the Jews considered idolatrous. In Caesarea and in Jerusalem Herod built theatres and amphitheatres. Games were held in both places every fourth year in honour of Augustus. The naked competitors greatly offended the Jews, as did the religious customs linked with the games. Worst of all, over the great gate of the temple in Jerusalem Herod placed a massive golden eagle – the symbol of Roman dominion.

Roman soldiers were stationed in Judea to keep in check the Parthians who came from an area north-east of Syria. They were never completely conquered by the Romans. The soldiers also kept the peace in Judea, prevented riots and ensured the safety of trade routes.

The army's headquarters was at Caesarea but a detachment was kept as a garrison in Jerusalem. Soldiers were always on duty in the outer temple area, and more were sent to Jerusalem at Passover time when pilgrims flocked to the city.

The Jews were left under no illusion as to who controlled their country. Uniformed soldiers were an everyday sight in their streets. The Jews were, however, exempt from military service because their law forbade the carrying of weapons on the sabbath, and because soldiers were expected to take part in pagan religious ceremonies.

One of the most hated aspects of Roman domination was the heavy taxation. The provinces were expected to bear most of the cost of administering the empire. In the province of Syria income tax was 1 per cent of a man's income per year, but there were also export and import taxes, taxes levied on crops – one-tenth of the grain crop and one-fifth of the wine, fruit and oil – purchase taxes, taxes payable on the transfer of property, emergency taxes, and so on.

A Roman official called a censor was responsible for collecting the revenue but he sold the right to extort it to the highest bidders. These tax collectors demanded more money than was due and kept the difference for themselves. It is likely that they took bribes from the rich so it was the poor people who really paid for the Roman government.

There were frequent Jewish revolts against the Romans, triggered by ill-treatment of the Jews. In the time of the procurator Ventidius Cumanus (AD 48–52) a Roman soldier threw a scroll of the Law into the fire. The Jews were so incensed that Cumanus was forced to have the soldier executed. Under Judas the Galilean the Jews revolted against the excessive taxes but the revolt was put down with great cruelty and all the rebels were executed (Acts 5:37). Because they longed to be free of Rome sects such as the Zealots openly rebelled, and the Essenes opted out of normal citizenship in their self-supporting community.

The occupation had some benefits. The Romans secured peace and built a good system of roads. This in turn encouraged trade. They often respected local customs, allowed religious freedom and a certain degree of self-government. They built baths and government offices. The Sanhedrin, (the Jewish council of seventy elders and the high priest which met in Jerusalem) had control of religious affairs and also administered government and justice under the authority of the Roman procurator. Although it tried certain criminal cases it does not seem to have had the right to enforce capital punishment, which is why Jesus had to be executed by Pilate, the Roman governor.

Titus' soldiers parade the seven-branched lampstand taken from the temple.

Resistance to a ruling power has often taken the form of guerrilla warfare. The Zealots used similar tactics in their attempt to regain Jewish national independence.

The Zealots

The census ordered by Augustus through his legate Quirinius mentioned in the Gospel story of Jesus' birth, was the first step for the assessment of taxes. Augustus is known to have ordered similar censuses periodically in Egypt.

In AD 6 Quirinius ordered a second census in Judea. This provoked an unsuccessful revolt led by Judas of Galilee. This marked the birth of the resistance movement of nationalists, later called the Zealots. This group refused to pay taxes to the Romans and were prepared to kill both Romans and Jewish collaborators.

Jesus had a former Zealot, Simon, as a disciple and was himself crucified as a political agitator. For these reasons some scholars have suggested that Jesus sympathized with the Zealot movement. This overlooks the fact that another disciple, Matthew, was a former tax-collector. Far from following Zealot policy, Jesus, when shown a coin with the image of Caesar, said: 'Pay the Emperor what belongs to the Emperor.'

Matthew 22: 15-22

When the sons of Judas of Galilee raised a rebellion, they were crucified by Tiberius Alexander, governor of Judea. During the governorship of Fadus a man called Theudas claimed that he could cause the River Jordan to part. While Felix was governor a false prophet from Egypt gathered several thousand followers on the Mount of Olives. The apostle Paul was mistaken for this Egyptian by the Roman officer who rescued him from a riot in the temple precincts.

AD 46–48
AD 44–46

Acts 21: 38

It was under Felix that radical Zealots, called *Sicarii* from the concealed daggers they used to assassinate their victims, first made their appearance and assassinated the high priest. The growth of the Zealot nationalist movement, together with the increasingly hardline policy of the Roman governors Albinus (62–64) and Florus (64–65), led to the outbreak of the First Jewish Revolt in 66.

Revolution

Josephus: AD 37–
about 100

Josephus, a priest and descendant of the Hasmonean family, is the main historian on whom we depend for the story of the Jews of the first century. His monumental work, *The Jewish Antiquities*, first published in 94, tells the history of the Jews from Old Testament times to his own day. His *Contra Apion* defended Judaism against the attacks of an anti-Semitic intellectual from Alexandria. As both his *Autobiography* and the vivid and invaluable *Jewish War* are written to defend his own conduct, they are undoubtedly coloured by his self-serving bias. Josephus had originally served as commander of the Jewish forces in Galilee, but in 67 had surrendered to the Romans under suspicious circumstances at Jotapata.

The Jewish Revolt was doomed to failure not only by the superior weight of Rome's legions but by the bitter rivalries within the Zealot factions, which inflicted more casualties upon each other than upon the Romans. According to the historian Eusebius, the Christians were advised to flee Jerusalem and go to Pella, just south of the Sea of Galilee, in Transjordan. As news of the revolt spread, fighting broke out between Jews and Gentiles in Syria and Egypt too. Tens of thousands of Jews were massacred.

In Palestine itself the Jews were at first surprisingly successful. They wiped out the Roman twelfth legion in the Beth-Horon pass west of Jerusalem, on its way from Syria. Alarmed at the news, Nero dispatched his best general, Vespasian, from Britain. Joining Vespasian's fifth and tenth legions was his son Titus with the fifteenth legion from Egypt. These combined forces subdued Galilee.

In June 68 Nero was assassinated, and chaos ensued with the succession of three emperors in a year. In 69 Vespasian was hailed by his own troops as emperor. He left Palestine for Rome and placed Titus in charge of the war. After a siege lasting five months the walls of Jerusalem were breached and the temple destroyed in 70, never to be rebuilt. Excavations in Jerusalem between 1968 and 1976 uncovered the magnificent architectural fragments which were hurled down from the parapets during the Roman attack upon the temple.

Josephus reports that over a million Jews were killed and about 100,000 taken prisoner. The Romans celebrated their victory in a series of coins which showed a weeping woman beneath a palm tree, the symbol of Judea. These coins were issued between 69 and 73, and then as commemorative issues in 77 and 78. The tenth legion was stationed permanently in Jerusalem; numerous examples of its stamped tiles have been discovered there.

Jews throughout the Empire were forced to divert their former temple offerings to Rome as a 'Jewish tax' for the temple of Jupiter there. The Emperor Domitian had a ninety-year old man publicly exposed to see if he was a circumcised Jew, and therefore liable to pay this tax.

Masada

The fortress of Masada stands on a rocky plateau, 1,400 feet (434 metres) above the western shore of the Dead Sea. According to tradition this cliff top was first fortified by Jonathan, the brother of Judas Maccabeus, during the struggle against the Seleucids. Herod the Great chose it as the site for a refuge for himself. The plateau was enclosed on all sides by a wall incorporating thirty towers and four gates.

Two aqueducts and a large number of deep cisterns were constructed which provided sufficient water for everyday needs. They also supplied fountains, the various bath-houses and even water for the gardens.

Excavations have shown that there were four groups of palace buildings. Some of them were probably residences of high officials, and administrative centres, baths, storehouses, workshops and barracks. Most spectacular was the palace built in three tiers on the northern edge of the cliff. It was used for entertainment and relaxation. A staircase connected the three terraces. Rows of columns supported the roofs of the buildings, the walls were decorated with frescoes or geometric and floral patterns, and many of the floors were of mosaic.

After the death of Herod the Great a Roman garrison was stationed at Masada. In AD 66, at the start of the Jewish revolt, it was captured by the Zealots. They adapted Herod's palaces as living quarters and command posts.

discovered. The Zealots built ritual baths and bathing pools, and a synagogue which faced Jerusalem. It was a rectangular building with four tiers of benches along the walls for the congregation.

Towards the end of the revolt many families fled for safety to Masada. Huts of mud and small stones were built for them, mainly around the edges of existing buildings. After the destruction of Jerusalem in AD 70 Masada remained the last rebel stronghold. But in AD 72 the Tenth Roman Legion with

Architectural features which were ornamental rather than useful were dismantled and used as additional building material. Partitions were put up in the large rooms to divide them into living quarters for several families. Even the rooms in the wall were used as living quarters. Remains of ovens were found in most of the rooms.

Some of the Zealots had come from the wealthy class of society. In one of the buildings remains of alabaster and gold vessels and hoards of coins were

thousands of auxiliary troops marched on it. Eight camps were set up and a siege wall 3 miles (4½ km) long was built around Masada to prevent any of the rebels escaping. A huge assault ramp was built of earth and the Romans finally breached the walls in AD 73. But rather than surrender, the Zealots had collected their personal belongings together and burned them. Then they chose ten men to kill every family until all 960 defenders were dead, except two women and five children who escaped by hiding in a cave.

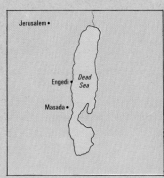

Above right: the three terraces of Herod's summer palace at Masada, seen here from the air.

Jerusalem falls

There were serious Jewish uprisings at Cyrenaica (in Libya), in Egypt, and Cyprus between 115–17, during the reign of the Emperor Trajan. On Cyprus the Jews are said to have killed 240,000 Gentiles. As a consequence Jews were banned from the island.

The last major Jewish revolt was led by Bar Cochba in 131–35, during the reign of the Emperor Hadrian. Unfortunately we have no eye-witness accounts of this war. According to the writer Dio Cassius, Hadrian, who loved Greek culture, proposed to make Jerusalem a Hellenistic city, and forbade the Jewish rite of circumcision.

Despite the Bar Cochba revolt, and sustained resistance by the Jews, Jerusalem was captured by the Romans in 134, and the last fortress, Bettar, southwest of Jerusalem, fell in 135. Hadrian rebuilt Jerusalem as a pagan city called Aelia Capitolina, and forbade Jews, including Jewish Christians, from entering it.

AD 361–63

Later when Jews were permitted to return it was to lament the destruction of the temple at the Wailing Wall – which we know was attested as early as 333. There was an attempt to rebuild the temple, encouraged by the Emperor Julian the Apostate, but this was frustrated by an earthquake or explosion. Archaeologists recently found a quotation from Isaiah 66:14 carved on the wall during this period: an expression of hope for the temple's re-erection.

Jerusalem seen from the Mount of Olives. The view is dominated by the Dome of the Rock, the Muslim mosque which stands on the site of Herod's temple.

The Bar Cochba revolt

The famous rabbi Akiba proclaimed the messianic pretender Bar Kosiba as Bar Cochba 'Son of the Star', in reference to an Old Testament prophecy that a 'star of Jacob' would crush Israel's oppressors. Bar Cochba's revolt was so widespread that the Romans called in the third and the twenty-second legions to aid the sixth and the tenth legions already in Palestine, removing troops from the German and Danube frontiers in the process. In the fighting the twenty-second legion was annihilated. The Emperor Hadrian sent his best commanders to help including Julius Severus, the governor of

Britain. Instead of engaging Bar Cochba's warriors in open warfare, the Romans rounded up groups of rebels and besieged them. Thousands died from hunger and thirst. Dio Cassius, the third-century historian, states that 985 settlements and fifty fortresses were destroyed by the Romans.

The revolt was put down with such cruelty that whole families fled and hid in caves. This fact was known to Jerome (345–419) but has recently been confirmed by archaeological expeditions which explored caves in the Judean desert, west of the Dead Sea, in 1960 and 1961.

Remains of Roman camps were found on both the northern and southern cliffs of the canyon. Soldiers were stationed there to prevent the Jews escaping from the caves below.

In 1960 and 1961 Yigael Yadin led expeditions to excavate the 'Cave of the Letters'. Below: the main entrance to the cave was reached by climbing a rope ladder secured by a member of the team.
Below right: members of the team in hall A, one of three halls in the cave.

The Cave of the Letters

About 110 yards (100 metres) below the Roman camp are the two entrances to the 'Cave of the Letters'. There are three large caverns linked by natural corridors. From the finds made in them a picture of life during the revolt has been put together.

The first clear piece of evidence to show that the cave was occupied during Bar Cochba's time was a coin found just outside one entrance. On one side was stamped 'Simeon' – Bar Cochba's first name – and on the other 'of the freedom of Jerusalem', showing how the Jews longed for their independence. The cave must have been the hiding-place of several families. Their bones were found in heaps, presumably collected by relatives who came to the cave after the Romans had left.

The most spectacular discovery was of fifteen letters from Bar Cochba himself. Most were written in the first person, but had obviously been dictated in the three languages used in Judea at the time – Aramaic, Hebrew and Greek. They were all written on papyrus except one on a wooden slat.

One letter requested supplies

Engedi ■

Roman camp

Entrances to the Cave of the Letters

Dead Sea

Nahal Hever

□ −1,000 ft/300 m
▨ 0 ft/0 m

Scale ├─┤ 1 mile
        ├─┤ 1 km

for the Feast of Tabernacles. The rest of the correspondence was addressed to Bar Cochba's commanders in the En-gedi region. They were given orders to punish anyone who disobeyed them. He asked for reinforcements to be sent to him, and also for supplies of salt and grain.

But the loyalty and support of these commanders seem to have wavered. When they failed to deal properly with the cargo of a ship which had docked at En-gedi he wrote: 'In comfort you sit, eat and drink from the property of the House of Israel, and care nothing for your brothers.'

Families who fled to the caves during the Bar Cochba revolt took their precious possessions with them. The beautiful glass bowl (below) had been packed in palm fibre for protection. Other finds (right) included a willow basket, wool used for mending, a glass container used for cosmetic oil, a necklace made of semi-precious stones and a mirror held in a wooden case. The bowl and jugs (bottom right) were part of a collection of nineteen bronze objects taken from the Romans, discovered in a basket (bottom left). Pagan faces on the jug handles had been scratched out to make them acceptable to their Jewish owners.

Hebrew and Aramaic

In the period between the writing of the Old and New Testaments **Hebrew** was replaced as the everyday language of the Jews by Aramaic. But the rabbis continued to use Hebrew in their learned deliberations, as we see from the *Mishnah*, the book of law written in that language. The majority of the Essene sect documents found among the Dead Sea Scrolls were written in Hebrew. When the actual words spoken are quoted in the New Testament they are often Aramaic, not Hebrew.

Aramaic is a Semitic language, originally used by the Aramaeans of Syria, which became widespread throughout the Near East as an international language. Because its alphabet was easier to use than the cumbersome cuneiform scripts used by the Assyrians and the Persians, they adopted it for diplomacy and commerce.

Imperial Aramaic (700–200 BC) was quite uniform and is found on inscriptions from as far afield as Anatolia and Afghanistan. Some passages in

Top: a modern Hebrew scribe.

Above: a fifth-century BC fragment of Aramaic writing.

the Old Testament books of Ezra and of Daniel are written in this dialect.

Other periods and dialects included:

Middle Aramaic (200 BC–AD 200). After Alexander the Great had conquered the Near East and Greek had spread widely, various local dialects of Aramaic developed. From this period comes the Aramaic of the New Testament, of some of the Dead Sea Scrolls, of the Bar Cochba texts, of the Nabataeans and of the Palmyreneans.

Late Aramaic (AD 200–700). In this era the western branch of Aramaic included Samaritan, and Christian Palestinian Aramaic; the eastern branch included Syriac, Babylonian Talmudic Aramaic and Mandaic.

When Jesus cried out on the cross 'My God, my God, why did you abandon me?' (*Eloi, Eloi, lama sabachthani*), he was speaking Aramaic. Many words in the New Testament are transliterations from the Aramaic. Peter's name Cephas is from *kēphā*, 'rock'; Thomas is from *tōmā*, 'twin'; *Bar*, the Aramaic word for 'son' occurs in such names as Bartholomew, Bar-Jonas, Barabbas and Bartimaeus. (The Hebrew word for son is *ben*.) Golgotha is from *golgoltā* 'skull'; and Maranatha comes from *māran* 'our Lord' and *etā* 'come'.

Apart from some of the Dead Sea Scrolls, and the Bar-Cochba

texts, only one extensive writing in Aramaic survives from Palestine in the New Testament period – the *Megillat Tacanit* 'The Scroll of Fasting'. Almost all other Aramaic texts surviving are short inscriptions on the limestone boxes used for the deposit of the bones of the dead (ossuaries) dating from 100 BC to AD 70. Of the twenty-nine inscribed ossuaries recovered on the Mount of Olives by one archaeologist, eleven were in Aramaic, seven in Hebrew and eleven in Greek.

Some time after the exile of the Jews to Babylon, Aramaic translations and paraphrases of the Hebrew Scriptures, called *targums*, were made for those who understood Aramaic better than Hebrew. We have *targums* for all the Old Testament books except Daniel, Ezra and Nehemiah. The earliest extant *targums* are from Qumran on the Dead Sea. An extensive *targum* on portions of Job came from one cave and dates from 150–100 BC.

The major *targum* of the first five books of the Old Testament, the Pentateuch, is known as *Onkelos*. It is quite a literal translation of the Hebrew and seems to have originated in Palestine, but was later edited in Babylonia between the second and fifth centuries AD. The major *targum* of the books of the prophets is known as *Jonathan*. It was modelled on *Onkelos*, but is a less literal translation.

Jewish religious sects

Samaritans

When the Assyrians conquered the ten northern tribes of Israel they deported many of the inhabitants in 722 BC. Foreigners from Mesopotamia and Syria were imported to replace them. These people inter-married with the Jews who were left to form the mixed race of Samaritans.

Nehemiah 4

In 445 BC the Jewish leader Nehemiah rejected the Samaritans' offer to help rebuild the walls of Jerusalem. He then had to face opposition from their governor, Sanballat, but fulfilled his task by keeping an armed guard on duty.

The breach between the Jews and the Samaritans widened when the Samaritans built a separate temple on Mount Gerizim, under a later Sanballat. The Samaritans not only differed from the Jews in worshipping on Mount Gerizim but also in accepting only the first five books of the Old Testament as Scripture. In 128 BC the Jewish leader John Hyrcanus destroyed the Samaritan temple.

Luke 10: 29-37

In Jesus' day there was bitter hostility between the Samaritans and the Jews. The Samaritans sometimes waylaid Jewish pilgrims passing through their territory. On the other hand, for most Jews there could be no such thing as a 'good' Samaritan.

Today the Samaritans, who number only about 500, are the only quasi-Jewish sect which still actually slaughter sheep at the Passover; Jews cannot do this without their temple.

Jews from Galilee had to pass through the hilly country of Samaria in order to reach Jerusalem.

Pharisees

The name of the Pharisees literally means 'separated ones'. Their roots go back to the movement of 'the pious' (Hebrew *Hasidim*) who with the Maccabees, opposed attempts to introduce Greek elements into Jewish culture in the second century BC. Later they opposed the Maccabees when they combined secular and religious offices.

Jonathan: 160–143 BC

The Pharisees are first mentioned as a distinct group under the high priest Jonathan. Unlike the Essenes, who looked for a kingdom of the new age, the Pharisees were willing to make compromises in order to survive as a distinct group. For this they were branded 'hypocrites' by the Essenes. On the other hand, as the Pharisees firmly believed in the resurrection, they clashed with the Sadducees. They held that 'he that says there is no resurrection of the dead has no share in the world to come'. The Sadducees were mainly priests, concerned with the temple worship practices; the Pharisees were primarily scribes, who interpreted the scriptures according to the oral law, which they held was as ancient as the written Law.

Their concern in interpreting the Law (the *Torah*) was first of all to apply the eternal Law to the changing circumstances of their day, by means of elaborate arguments. Secondly, they sought to 'make a hedge about the Law', that is, to take added precautions to prevent the breaking of the Law. For example, if the Law said that a task must be completed by morning, the rabbis went a step further and said that it should be completed by the previous midnight. A tailor should not place a needle in his clothes on Friday for fear he carry it with him and break the sabbath law. It was this punctilious zeal for the letter of the Law

Matthew 23: 1-28

which was condemned by Jesus as hypocrisy.

Not all Pharisees were hypocrites, however. In the generation before Jesus, Hillel, a famous rabbi who was

An orthodox Jew saying his morning prayers. On his forehead is a phylactery containing extracts of the Law – a literal interpretation of the command to bind the Law to himself.

originally from Babylonia, said: 'Do not do to others that which is hateful to you.' Hillel's grandson, Gamaliel, was the most famous rabbi of his day. The apostle Paul studied under him, and was until his conversion to Christianity a zealously sincere Pharisee.

The Pharisees were also opposed to the revolutionary policy of the Zealots. The Pharisee leader Johanan ben Zakkai secured permission from the Emperor Vespasian to open a rabbinical school at Jamnia (Jabneh) near Jaffa, which enabled Pharisaism to survive the Jewish-Roman War.

The Mishnah and the Talmud

The Pharisaic rabbis spent much time making oral comments on the Law. Those made in the first two centuries AD were compiled by Judah Hanasi about AD 200 to form the important collection known as the *Mishnah*. These rabbis were known as the *Tannaim* or 'Teachers' and were chiefly concerned with decisions about regulations. A less important collection of their comments is known as the *Tosefta* or 'Enlargement'.

The later expositions on the *Mishnah* by the 'Expositors' (*Amoraim*) of Palestine and of Babylonia were known collectively as the *Gemara* or 'Completion'. The combined text of the *Mishnah* and the related *Gemara* is known as the *Talmud*. These Pharisaic traditions form the basis of orthodox Judaism today.

Sermons commenting on the scriptures, known as *Midrashim*, were also compiled. The earlier Tannaitic *Midrashim* were mainly concerned with regulations. They included commentaries on Exodus, Leviticus, Numbers and Deuteronomy.

The later Amoraic *Midrashim* include much folklore and legendary materials. The greatest collection, the *Midrash Rabbah*, was not compiled until the sixth or seventh century AD. It includes commentaries on both the five books of the Law (the *Pentateuch*), and the five 'scrolls' of Canticles, Ruth, Lamentations, Ecclesiastes and Esther.

Essenes The Essenes are not mentioned by name in the New Testament but are known from the writings of Josephus, Philo and Pliny the Elder. Most scholars identify them with the monastic community at Qumran which produced the Dead Sea Scrolls, first discovered in 1947.

Though there were married Essenes scattered in villages, the highest ideal was attained by the celibate community at Qumran. Members initiated into the community held property in common. They had repeated ritual immersions and took part in a common meal. They considered that the Sadducees were corrupt and the Pharisees lax in observing the ritual commandments.

According to their 'Damascus Document' the Essenes were

Matthew 5: 43

prepared to rescue a man from a pit on the sabbath only if they could do it without implements. The Pharisees, however, held that saving life was more important than sabbath observance. Jesus may have been referring to the Essenes when he spoke of those who taught that it was a duty to hate one's enemies.

The Dead Sea Scrolls group evidently expected two messiahs: a priestly messiah from the tribe of Levi, and a kingly messiah from the tribe of Judah. They believed that they were living in the last days before the final war between the sons of light and the sons of darkness. Their anonymous leader was the 'Teacher of Righteousness', one who was persecuted by the high priest.

Essenes from Qumran hid manuscripts from their library – the Dead Sea Scrolls – in these caves during the First Jewish War. A shepherd boy discovered the scrolls by chance in 1947.

Hyrcanus: 134–104 BC

Excavations at Khirbet Qumran between 1951 and 1956 revealed that the community settled there in the time of the Jewish leader Hyrcanus. At most 400 men lived at Qumran. The cemetery of over a thousand burials includes the skeletons of women and children, possibly members of married Essene families.

The Dead Sea Scrolls include Hebrew manuscripts of the Old Testament, which are a thousand years older than the Masoretic copies of the Hebrew text dating from the ninth century AD on which translators previously had to depend.

Comparison with the later documents shows that they were accurate copies. Other scrolls indicate that the *Septuagint*, the Greek translation of the Old Testament, may have been made from different Hebrew originals. A few manuscripts conform to the paraphrase-style of the Samaritan *Pentateuch*.

Among the scrolls are found for the first time Hebrew and Aramaic manuscripts of apocryphal works such as *Tobit* and *Ecclesiasticus* for which previously we had only Greek versions. Other works such as *Enoch*, *Jubilees* and an apocryphal *Genesis* have been found. Writings connected with the sect have also been discovered, and include the 'Damascus Document', a *Manual of Discipline*, thanksgiving hymns, commentaries, and *The War Scroll*. A puzzling copper scroll is a veritable treasure map of fabulous amounts of gold and silver.

Greek writings from Cave VII of the excavations have been identified as New Testament manuscripts by an eminent scholar, but they are too fragmentary to back up this claim.

There is no basis for the popular speculation that the Teacher of Righteousness was crucified and raised from the dead before Jesus. Since John the Baptist was ascetic and celibate, lived near Qumran and baptized his hearers, some writers have suggested that he may have been in contact with the Essenes. But John's baptism was a single rite, in contrast to the repeated washings of Qumran.

The monastery at Qumran, along with the Essene community, were both destroyed by the Romans in AD 68.

The Essenes' settlement on the shores of the Dead Sea. Excavations have revealed a writing-room, water cisterns, baths for ritual washings, a kitchen and several other rooms.

Sadducees

The Sadducees were so named because they claimed to be descended from Zadok, the high priest at the time of King David and King Solomon. They consisted of the wealthy aristocratic families who controlled the office of high priest. They rejected belief in angels and the resurrection, but they were not liberal rationalists. Rather, they were arch-conservatives, who observed the Law of the Books of Moses (Pentateuch) and who rejected later interpretations of the law, the 'oral law'.

The Sadducees were angered at Jesus' cleansing the temple and at his teaching on the resurrection. It was Sadducean chief priests who condemned Jesus at a night-time trial and handed him over to Pilate. The Sadducees were primarily responsible for trying to suppress the preaching of Peter and the other apostles when they proclaimed that Jesus had risen from the dead. As the destruction of the temple in AD 70 destroyed their reason for existence, the Sadducees did not survive this period.

Worship in a modern synagogue in Israel.

The synagogue

During the Babylonian exile in the sixth century BC Jews began gathering to pray and study the scriptures in the synagogue. A quorum of ten men was necessary to form a synagogue. Women sat in a separate section, and were not expected to take part.

Numerous synagogues were set up in Jerusalem, including one for freedmen, or ex-slaves. The well-preserved synagogue at Capernaum dates only from the third or fourth century AD but almost certainly stands on the site of the building where Jesus spoke. About the only synagogue visible today which dates to the first century AD is the building excavated at Masada.

Wherever the apostle Paul travelled he made first for the local synagogue to preach the Christian message to the Jews. As a qualified rabbi he would be invited to expound the weekly readings from the *Torah* and the Prophets. At Philippi he went to 'a place of prayer'. This was a common description for a synagogue and may have been a synagogue rather than just a riverside place of prayer, as is

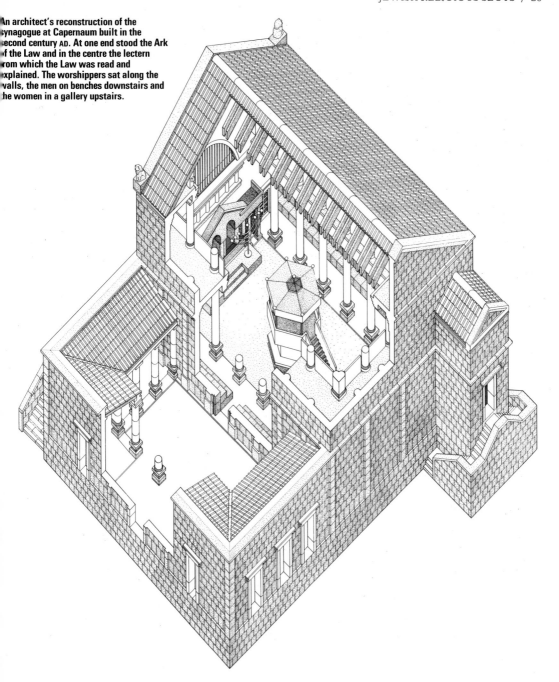

traditionally accepted.

Some synagogues were huge. Excavators have discovered an enormous synagogue at Sardis, in western Turkey, which was in use from AD 200 to 600. The main hall is 60 metres/65 yards long, with a forecourt and porch projecting an additional 40 metres/43 yards. The great Diploston synagogue in Alexandria was so enormous that a man was stationed in the middle of the building so he could signal with a flag the correct moment for the Amen to people at the back of the building.

Jews across the Empire

The Jewish historian Josephus writes of three million pilgrims converging on Jerusalem during the Passover celebrations, and of over a million killed during the First Jewish-Roman War. These figures may be grossly exaggerated; one modern scholar puts the number of pilgrims at 125–150,000 and the permanent population of Jerusalem at 25–55,000; a second estimates Jerusalem's population at 150,000; and a third suggests that there was a total of half a million Jews in Palestine as a whole. The total population of the Roman Empire has been guessed at from fifty-five to eighty million, with the heaviest concentration in eastern cities.

Clearly many more Jews were dispersed outside Palestine than lived within it. A great variety of Jews from throughout the Empire were pilgrims in Jerusalem on the Day of Pentecost, and such people are often called Jews of the dispersion, or the *diaspora*.

Acts 2: 5-13

Jews across the Empire

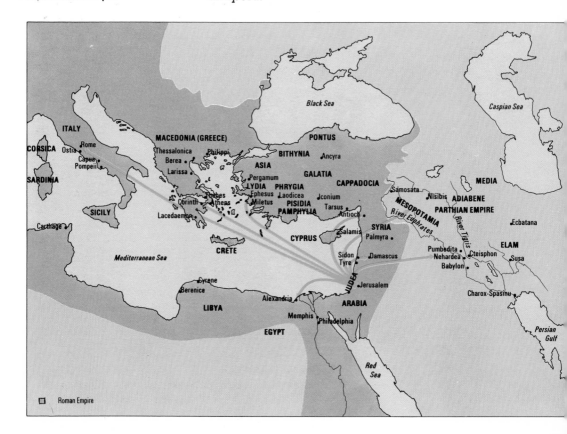

Roman Empire

Large numbers of Jews settled in Egypt in the third century BC when Judea was ruled by the Egyptian Ptolemaic kings. At that time this pyramid at Saqqara had already been standing over 2,000 years.

The worldwide distribution of the Jews is also reflected in the epitaphs of those who were buried at Jerusalem and Beth Shearim. They mention Jews from Palmyra in Syria, Cyrene in Libya, Lacedaemon in Greece, Delos in the Aegean, Capua in Italy, and many other places.

Jews in Egypt

According to the writer Philo there were a million Jews out of a total Egyptian population of eight-and-a-half million, though this may be an exaggerated figure. It is certain, however, that two out of the five districts of the great city of Alexandria were Jewish. Second only to Rome, Alexandria had a total population of over 300,000.

Philo: AD 20–50

It was from Alexandria, the intellectual centre of the Hellenistic world, that the great Jewish writer, Philo, came. He knew no Hebrew, and explained the Old Testament on the principles of Greek philosophy, interpreting it by allegory. He suggested that there was an intermediary between God and man called 'the Word' (*Logos*), an idea which may have influenced the writer of John's Gospel and certainly influenced later Christian thinkers.

The Jews in Alexandria had a self-governing community but not the full rights of citizenship, despite the claims of Josephus to the contrary. There was constant friction between the Jews and the 'Greeks' of Alexandria. When Agrippa I visited the city in AD 38, full-scale riots broke out during which 400 Jewish houses were destroyed. Philo went to the Emperor Gaius Caligula to protest about the behaviour of the governor, Flaccus. Caligula dismissed the Jewish appeal with contempt: 'It seems to me that people who are stupid enough not to believe that I have become a god are more to be pitied than condemned.' But later, at the request of his friend Agrippa, Caligula had Flaccus executed.

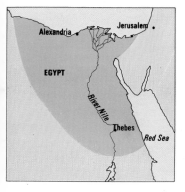

Looking towards Cairo, capital of modern
Egypt.

Claudius: AD 41–54

Further disturbances arose between the Jews and other
Alexandrians under the Emperor Claudius, who warned in a
letter: 'I order that the Alexandrians show themselves tolerant
and kindly towards the Jews who for many years have lived in
the same city . . . I explicitly order the Jews not to agitate for
more privileges . . . not to force their way into games at the
gymnasia.'

Philo's brother, Alexander the Alabarch, was officially
responsible for the collection of taxes. He was one of the
wealthiest men in the world, and a friend of Claudius. He
provided silver and gold plates for the gates of the Jewish
temple in Jerusalem.

Alexander's son, Tiberius Julius Alexander, turned his back
upon his Jewish culture and religion, to advance to the highest
status among the Romans. From AD 46 to 48 he served as the
governor of Judea, and was the governor of Egypt in 66, when
the Jewish-Roman War broke out. He was in fact responsible
for setting the Roman soldiers against his fellow Jews, 50,000 of
whom were killed. He was the first important Roman official to
hail Vespasian as emperor in 69, and served as chief-of-staff
under Titus at the siege of Jerusalem.

Syrian Jews

Acts 9: 1-3

Saul set out for Damascus in his zeal to persecute Christians
before his conversion to Christ, with letters from the high
priest addressed to various synagogues of the city. Although
his conversion prevented his intended massacre, during the
First Jewish-Roman War 10,500 of his fellow Jews were killed
in Damascus (or 18,000 according to another passage in
Josephus).

It is estimated that of the 300,000 people in the third largest city in the Empire, Antioch on the Orontes, about 12 per cent were Jews. Excavations between 1932 and 1939, however, uncovered only one inscription and a marble fragment which gave evidence of the Jewish community. At the suburb of Daphne, 5 miles south of Antioch, archaeologists found the Roman theatre which the Emperor Vespasian built on the site of the Jewish synagogue.

In Roman times a large group of Jews lived here at Palmyra, an oasis town on an important trade route across the Syrian Desert. These ruins are of the splendid colonnaded street and triumphal arch built during Hadrian's reign.

Jews in Turkey and Greece

The first major settlement of Jews in Anatolia (Turkey) was arranged by the Seleucid ruler Antiochus III, when he moved 2,000 Jewish families from Mesopotamia to Lydia and Phrygia in 200 BC. He promised them religious freedom, gave them lands, and exempted their harvests from taxation for ten years.

In 62 BC Lucius Valerius Flaccus, Roman governor of Asia

The altar to Zeus at Pergamum, one of the cities in Anatolia (Turkey) where Jews settled. Despite contact with other religions the Jews retained their own beliefs.

(western Turkey) confiscated the gold which the Jews had collected to send to Jerusalem. When he was brought to trial on charges of extortion in 59 BC the governor was defended by Hortensius and Cicero, the two leading advocates of the day. In his speech Cicero remarked of the Jews: 'You know how large a group they are, how unanimously they stick together, how influential they are in politics.'

In Greece, the apostle Paul found Jews in the three major cities of Macedonia – Philippi, Thessalonica and Berea – and a small Jewish community at Athens. He spent much of his time with the strategic Jewish community of Corinth. Corinth had a harbour at Lechaeum on the west coast of the neck of land on which it was built, and one on the east coast, Cenchreae. Ships' captains preferred to have their ships dragged across the neck of land rather than risk the dangerous voyage around the southern Peloponnesus.

In 1898 a fragment of an inscription was found in the agora, or city-centre of Corinth which refers to a 'synagogue of the Hebrews'. This may have belonged to the later building which stood on the site of the synagogue where Paul preached.

Jews in Mesopotamia

Many Jews failed to return to Palestine with Zerubbabel or Ezra after the exile in Babylon so that the roots of the Jewish community in Mesopotamia go back to the sixth century BC. Unfortunately there is little evidence for the development of Judaism in this important area until about AD 220, but it is known that the Jewish communities in Mesopotamia fell under the Parthians who conquered this area in 140 BC. Some writers have suggested that Judaism came under the influence of the Persian religion of Zoroastrianism at this time, but there is no evidence for this. The Jews in Mesopotamia collected together their annual temple contributions at Nehardea in the south, and at Nisibis in the north, and sent them in armed convoys to Jerusalem.

Artabanus: AD 16–44

During the reign of the weak Parthian king, Artabanus III, two Jewish brothers in Nehardea, called Asinaeus and Anilaeus, succeeded in setting up a semi-independent Jewish state owing allegiance to him for about fifteen years. But when this state was put down, some 50,000 Jews were killed.

A Jewish merchant at Charax-Spasinu, on the Persian Gulf, converted Izates, the prince of Adiabene (ancient Assyria), and his mother Helena, who was also converted to Judaism, built a palace in Jerusalem. During the famine of AD 46–48 she bought grain in Egypt and figs in Cyprus to feed the people of Jerusalem. She was buried in Jerusalem in a splendid tomb, closed with a rolling stone, which is still visible.

Very little is known about the other Jewish communities further east in Persia.

The River Euphrates is the southern boundary of Mesopotamia.

Jews in Italy

The Jews and the Romans first made official contact in 161 BC when Judas Maccabeus formed an alliance with Rome. In 139 BC the controller of aliens expelled from Rome astrologers and 'Jews who attempted to damage the morals of the Romans with the worship of Jupiter Sabazius'. As Sabazius is the name of a Phrygian god, this may be a confused reference to the Jewish *Jehovah Sabaoth* ('Lord of Hosts').

In 61 BC Pompey brought back to Rome with him Jewish prisoners. According to Philo, they were later freed and formed the nucleus of the Jewish community in Rome. This is unlikely, however, since Cicero in 59 BC wrote that the Jews were already numerous and influential.

During the Civil War between Pompey and Julius Caesar, the Jews came to the aid of Caesar. He granted the Jews special privileges as a 'recognized religion'. Jews were exempted from military conscription; they were allowed to settle their

The Colosseum at Rome. By the first century AD, when the Colosseum was built, Jews comprised at least 4 per cent of Rome's population.

Gaius Caligula, the mad emperor who claimed to be divine.

disputes in their own courts; grain was not distributed to them on the sabbath. They were permitted to send contributions of half a shekel (or two *denarii*) to Jerusalem. When the Romans developed the cult of emperor worship, Jews were excused from taking part in the rites, but had to pray for the emperor.

It has been estimated that by the first century AD there were about 40–60,000 Jews among the million people of Rome. After the death of King Herod the Great in 4 BC, about 8,000 Jews living in Rome protested against the appointment of Archelaus as his successor.

In AD 19 four Jewish tricksters created a scandal by fooling a wealthy female Jewish convert into giving them the gifts she had contributed to the temple. As a consequence the Emperor Tiberius sent 4,000 Jewish freedmen to labour on the notoriously unhealthy island of Sardinia. The mad Emperor Gaius Caligula (AD 37–41) alarmed the Jews by proposing to erect a statue of himself in the Jewish temple in Jerusalem in spite of protests by his friend Agrippa I. This project was delayed by the reluctance of the Syrian governor Petronius, and was finally thwarted by the emperor's assassination.

Jews and Christians

The first Christians were Jews who had come to believe that Jesus was the Messiah for whom the Jewish nation had been waiting. They preached this message to Jews from Palestine and other parts of the Roman Empire, basing it on prophecies from the Old Testament.

When the Christians were forced to flee from Jerusalem in the wave of persecution which followed Stephen's death, they took their message with them. Soon people with no Jewish background ('Gentiles') were becoming members of the Christian church. One of the first places where this happened was Antioch, the third largest city of the Empire.

The apostle Peter came to realize that the Christian message was for everyone, not just for Jews, while he was at Joppa. Immediately afterwards he baptized

The Jewish quarter in Jerusalem. Rome replaced Jerusalem as the centre of Christianity after the First Jewish War of AD 66–70.

Cornelius, a non-Jewish centurion in the Roman army (Acts 10). When Peter reported back to the church in Jerusalem they agreed to accept both Jews and Gentiles.

By the time that Paul and Barnabas returned from their journey to Asia Minor such large numbers of Gentiles had become Christians that some Jewish Christians felt threatened. They believed that as Christianity had its roots in Judaism, Gentiles who became Christians should be made to keep the Jewish Law. About AD 49 a council was held in Jerusalem to discuss the matter (Acts 15: 1-21). Paul argued strongly that the Gentiles should not have to do something which the Jews themselves had found impossible: people could not find God by keeping the Jewish Law, but only by faith in Jesus Christ. The council decided to ask non-Jewish Christians only to abstain from certain foods of which the Jews disapproved, and to keep the moral code. There were no longer any barriers between races in the church.

For some years after Jesus, Jewish Christians still worshipped in the synagogues on the sabbath (Saturday) as well as meeting together on Sunday, the day that Jesus rose from the dead. Paul often used the synagogue as a base for his preaching when he visited a new town. Christians also continued to read and quote from the Old Testament.

But many Jews regarded Christians as heretics who were a threat to Judaism. When Herod Agrippa I wanted to please some Jewish leaders he persecuted the Christians, killing James and arresting Peter. Paul was attacked at several places, including Lystra and Thessalonica, by Jews who were alarmed at the number of converts he was making. The Roman authorities treated Christians as a Jewish sect and only intervened in disputes between Christians and Jews if the public peace was threatened. Only when Nero had blamed Christians for the fire which destroyed much of Rome in AD 64 was it recognized that a new religion had emerged.

In the First Jewish War of AD 66–70 Christians from Jerusalem fled to Pella, about 60 miles north-east of the city. Because they refused to take an active part in the fight against the Romans they became even more despised by the Jews. About AD 90 a new centre of Jewish learning was founded at Jamnia, and new rules concerning Judaism were made. Christians were forbidden to worship in the synagogues and were even cursed in the prayers. Christianity and Judaism had become totally separate.

MYTHS AND CULTS

By the time of the Hellenistic period, in the third and second centuries BC, most people no longer had a naive faith in the Greek gods who appeared in human form, such as Zeus and Hera. But as late as the first century AD rural peasants of Lystra (in modern Turkey) could still mistake Paul and Barnabas as Zeus and Hermes in human form. With the development of philosophy in the sixth century BC, Greek intellectuals began to regard the myths as allegories. The thinker Xenophanes went so far as to suggest that there was a single god who was totally unlike man.

But in addition to this rationalism, which the modern mind admires, there were always elements of irrationalism among the Greeks. Side by side with philosophy and logic were mystic cults which called forth unrestrained emotions

Greek religion

The first mystery cult

The oldest of the Greek mystery cults was celebrated at Eleusis, twelve miles west of Athens. This cult revolved around the myth of Demeter's daughter Persephone who was abducted by Hades and who had to spend four months underground each year. Those wanting initiation into the cult had to be Greek-speaking and innocent of murder.

The great festival took place in September. The initiates first bathed in the sea, then offered a sow in sacrifice. They then went in procession along the Sacred Way to Eleusis, drinking the alcoholic *kykeon*, made of roasted barley. The climax of the festival was reached at Eleusis. When it was dark the initiates were ushered into a building called the Telesterion, 53 metres/170 feet square. There the leader showed them an object, probably an ear of grain, amidst a scene filled with smoke and lights.

Emperors including Augustus, Hadrian and Marcus Aurelius, asked to be admitted into the Eleusinian rites, as these were the most prestigious. Nero's application, however was rejected. The Eleusinian ceremonies were continued until AD 395, when the barbarian Alaric invaded Greece.

The oldest Greek mystery cult, apart from Eleusis, was that

Greece

The site at Eleusis in Greece where, according to legend, Persephone was taken each year into the underworld by Hades.

of the Cabeiri, at Samothrace, an island off the northwest coast of Turkey. The Cabeiri were volcanic gods. The initiates met at night. Wearing crowns and bearing lamps, they viewed some mysterious spectacle. They were promised protection, especially from shipwreck.

Begun in the sixth century BC, the mysteries of the Cabeiri became popular especially among the Thracians and Macedonians in the Hellenistic age. Philip and Olympias, the parents of Alexander the Great, first met during one of the ceremonies. All classes were welcome, from Roman governors to slaves. The sanctuary at Samothrace was damaged by an earthquake in about AD 200 and declined after this.

The orgies of Dionysus

The god Dionysus, called Bacchus by the Romans, was a god of vegetation, especially of wine. According to Greek myth he was the son of Zeus and Semele. Soon after his birth he was torn to pieces by the Titans, members of a race of giants, so he had to be born a second time. According to later traditions, Dionysus travelled as far as Egypt and India. People who opposed him were either driven mad or torn to pieces by their relatives, a fate vividly depicted in Euripides' play, *The Bacchae*.

The followers of Dionysus, who were primarily women, were known as the *Maenads* or 'the mad ones'. After becoming drunk with wine they would dance ecstatically, fondling serpents. The climax of their orgies was reached with the rending of a living animal limb by limb. Arnobius, a

Christian writer, protested: 'To show yourselves full of the divinity and majesty of the god, you demolish with gory mouths the intestines of goats bleating for mercy.'

546–527 BC

It was in honour of Dionysus that dramatic festivals were first held on the slopes of the Acropolis in Athens. Both tragedies (*tragoidoi* or 'goat songs') and comedies (*komoidoi* or 'village songs') developed out of the Dionysus cult.

500–450 BC

The earliest evidence for the introduction of Bacchus into Italy comes from a cemetery at Cumae which was reserved for initiates to this cult. The movement became prominent at the beginning of the second century BC. In 186 BC the Senate arrested 7,000 adherents, many of whom were executed for alleged crimes. A decree was passed which severely regulated the cult and limited gatherings to not more than five persons, and then only after permission had been obtained from the Senate.

Despite such persecution the worship of Bacchus survived. The cult is vividly illustrated in the frescoes of the Villa of Mysteries at Pompeii. These depict women initiates viewing a mysterious object, possibly a phallus, and undergoing ritual whipping.

In the fourth century AD the writer Firmicus Maternus reported that the Cretans still 'rend a living bull with their teeth, and they simulate madness of soul as they shriek

The Greek Empire.
The red line indicates the extent of Alexander's Empire before his death in 323 BC. After his death, his generals fought for control of the Empire. Ptolemy and his successors ruled Egypt and Palestine until 198 BC. Seleucus founded a dynasty in Babylon, the eastern part of Alexander's Empire, and (after 281 BC) Asia Minor. In 275 BC Macedonia came under the control of Antigonus Gonatas, the first of the 'Antigonid' kings.

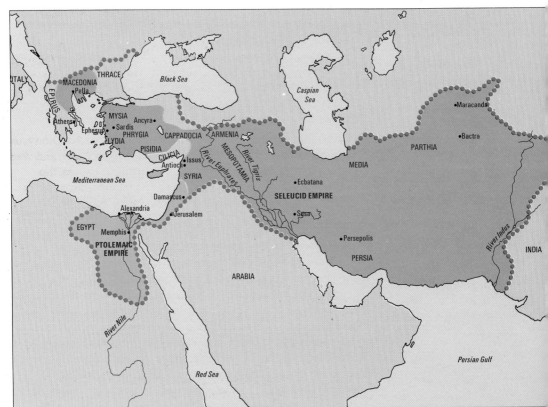

Orpheus plays his lyre to the animals and birds. This mosaic from the third century AD was discovered at Tarsus.

through the secret places of the forest with discordant clamours.'

This extraordinary cult has given a number of words to our language, including: 'ecstasy' (from *ekstasis* 'standing outside oneself'); 'enthusiasm' (derived from *entheos* 'indwelt by the god'); 'orgies' (from *orgia* 'rites'); and 'triumph' (derived from the Greek *thriambos* 'a hymn to Bacchus').

Orpheus and his cult

A separate religion based on an expanded legend of Dionysus was associated with the legendary musician Orpheus, and was known as Orphism. According to the Orphic writings, the Titans who killed Dionysus ate him except for his heart. With his heart Zeus created a new Dionysus, and destroyed the Titans. From the ashes of the Titans men were created, and so are creatures of a dual nature. Their bodies, which are derived from the Titans, are evil; but their souls, which are derived from Dionysus, are good. To achieve release from the cycle of reincarnation the Orphics went through purification, abstained from meat, and carefully controlled their behaviour.

Orphism originated sometime in the seventh and sixth centuries BC and became popular in the Hellenistic and Roman ages. Gold leaves found in tombs in Crete and southern Italy dating from the fourth and third century BC are probably Orphic. One of these leaves, from Thurii, reads: 'Pure I come hither from the pure, O divine mistress of Hades . . . By good fortune I have escaped the circle of burdensome care.'

The Olympian gods

The names of many of the Greek gods are well-known. Around them grew myths and legends about the intrigues between them and their exploits among men. Here are some of the more important of them.

Aphrodite
The goddess of love and beauty, who was probably related to the Asian goddesses of love, Ishtar and Astarte. Flowers sprang up wherever she walked, and

The Parthenon in Athens, the temple built in honour of Athena Parthenos, the city's patron goddess.
Above right: a frieze from the temple showing, from left to right, Isis, Hera and Zeus.

birds flew around her. She had the power to beguile even the wisest gods. She bore several children to Ares, among them Fear and Terror.

Apollo
A son of Zeus, he was the god of light, truth, music and prophecy. He killed the serpent Python, and having received the gift of prophecy from Pan established the oracle at Delphi, where advice, which was sometimes ambiguous, was given to those who sought it.

Artemis
A favourite goddess of many women, to whom they prayed for safe childbirth. She was goddess of the moon, and twin sister of Apollo. In Homer's *Iliad* she appears as

a huntress. In Ephesus an Asian fertility goddess was worshipped as Artemis, the Roman Diana.

Demeter
The goddess of fruit and grain on whom the survival of Greece depended. As the mother of Persephone, carried off into the underworld by Hades, she caused a famine because of her sorrow.

Hera
The wife of Zeus and goddess of marriage and families. She was a formidable character, the friend of Jason in the myth of the Argonauts.

Hephaestos
The god of fire and of craftsmen, who made magic things for both gods and men. He was neglected by Zeus and Hera, his parents, but the beautiful jewellery he made won back his mother's affection.

Poseidon
The brother of Zeus, he was god of seas and earthquakes. He gave the horse to mankind, an animal which provided food, clothing and above all transport. The Greeks prayed to him to protect sailors.

Zeus
He was the ruler of Mount Olympus, the dwelling-place of the gods, having overthrown Cronus his father with the aid of Cyclops, Giants and Titans. He was the god of the weather, and he guided men's fortunes.

Greek philosophy

Theories of Pythagoras

Greek philosophy began in the sixth century BC with speculations on the nature of the universe by thinkers now known as the pre-Socratics. Many of these early philosophers, such as Thales, Heraclitus and Anaxagoras, came from Ionia, the Greek settlements of western Turkey.

These philosophers assumed that the universe arose naturally from either a single eternal substance or a combination of such substances, for example water, air or fire. Some, such as Heraclitus thought that the basic reality was change. 'You cannot step into the same river twice', he said. Others held that change is an illusion; all things remain the same.

Pythagoras: 578–496 BC

One of the early Ionian philosophers, Pythagoras of Samos is best known today for his theorem of the right-angled triangle: that the square of the hypotenuse (the longest side) is equal to the sum of the squares of the other two sides. Pythagoras also discovered the relationship between numbers and musical scales, and believed that he could learn the secrets of nature by observing the order of the heavens. Pythagoreans were the first to suggest that the earth was round.

But Pythagoras was more than a philosopher and a mathematician; he was also a mystic. Leaving Samos in 538, he went to Croton in southern Italy, where he established a religious community of men and women. Like modern Hindus and Buddhists, Pythagoreans believed in reincarnation. To achieve the release of their souls from imprisonment in the body the Pythagoreans abstained from eating meat and beans, and observed other taboos, such as avoiding woollen clothes.

Apollonius of Tyana who died in AD 98 attempted to imitate Pythagoras. His life was written by Philostratus under the patronage of Julia Domna, the wife of Septimius Severus who was Roman Emperor at the beginning of the third century AD. Though there are many striking resemblances in this account of Apollonius' miracles and his trial to the life of Christ, Philostratus may not have written it as a deliberate counterblast to the Gospels. But it was unhistorical, although probably influenced by the Gospels.

Apollonius was in fact a modified Pythagorean who practised magic and who won the admiration of a number of pagans, including the Emperors Caracalla and Alexander Severus. The latter set up statues of Apollonius, Christ, Abraham and Orpheus, and revered them equally.

A statue of Pythagoras at Chartres Cathedral, France, dating from the twelfth century AD.

Socrates, whose ideas are reflected in
Plato's writings.

Numenius of Apamea, in the second century AD, drew upon
both Pythagoras and Plato, as well as the Old Testament. He
made the remarkable statement that 'Plato was just a Moses
talking Greek'. He also quoted the writings of Egyptians, Magi
(Persian wise men) and Brahmans from India.

The teachings of Numenius closely resemble those of the
famous Neoplatonist, Plotinus. He claimed that there was a
supreme God, the One; and a double-faced second God, who
contemplates the first God and who also rules the visible
universe. Unlike Plotinus he believed in the eternal existence
of matter and an evil cosmic soul. Like Pythagoras he believed
in the cycle of reincarnation. Numenius was unique in his
belief that man had two souls: a good soul derived from the
second God, and an irrational soul derived from the cosmic
soul.

Plato

Socrates (469–399 BC) circulated around Athens constantly
questioning men. He was not a philosopher with dogmatic
views, but one who changed the concern of philosophy from
the universe to man and how he behaves. The good life, he
held, can be taught only if we know what it is. Socrates was

Terms the philosophers used

Allegory A story in which the meaning lies not in the literal facts but in the things they symbolize.

Amorality A view of life which is unconcerned with questions of right and wrong.

Cosmos The universe seen as an orderly system, opposed to chance and chaos.

Deity The nature of God; a name for God.

Demiurge A Gnostic name for the creator of the material world, considered to be a much lower being than the Supreme God.

Dualism The idea that there are two forces in the world – light and dark, or good and evil – continually opposed to each other.

Ethics The science of principles governing behaviour and morals.

Hedonism The belief that pleasure is the chief good and purpose of life.

Manichaeans A Gnostic group founded by Mani (AD 216–76) who claimed to have received God's final revelation.

Mystery cults Religions with secret rites known only by those who had been initiated into them.

Mystics People who through meditation and self-discipline sought self-knowledge and spiritual revelation.

Nous The principle of objective thought, giving order and unity to things; the Supreme God, the source of all purposes.

Pantheism A religious or philosophical system which regards the physical world as a manifestation of God; God is not a being separate from everything and everyone else.

Providence The plan and provision of God for the world, sustaining the created order.

Rationalism The belief that human reason can understand the universe without additional revelation from God.

Reincarnation The belief that when a creature dies its soul passes into another body to work out the punishment or reward gained in earlier lives.

Soul The non-material aspect of human nature, supposed to have a divine origin; man's higher self.

Syllogism A form of argument in which a conclusion is deduced from two given statements which have a common term itself not forming part of the conclusion.

Theosophy A form of philosophy which claims that knowledge of God can be gained through trance or intuition.

accused of 'atheism' and of corrupting the Athenian youth. Some of his disciples, such as Alcibiades and Critias, did turn out to be notoriously bad characters. He was brought to trial in the Royal Stoa (which archaeologists have recently excavated) and condemned to death by drinking poisonous hemlock.

As Socrates himself wrote nothing that has survived, we depend for our information about him on the writings of his disciples such as Xenophon, and above all, Plato. Because Plato presents his own views in the form of dialogues with Socrates, it is not always easy to separate his own views from those of his master.

Plato: 428–347 BC

Plato established in 387 the first 'university' in a gymnasium on the outskirts of Athens known as the Academy. In an understandable reaction against the democracy which had condemned Socrates, Plato in his most famous work, *The Republic*, proposed an ideal state which was patterned more on the totalitarian state of Sparta than on Athens. He urged the censorship of the epics of Homer, the abolition of families, the education of women with men, and a selective process of training which would produce philosopher-rulers.

When an opportunity arose for Plato to put some of his

political ideas into practice in Syracuse (Sicily), he failed dismally. Sadder but wiser, Plato returned to more conservative ideas in his last work, *Laws*, restoring for example the place of the family.

Plato discusses the formation of the cosmos in the *Timaeus*, a work which profoundly influenced later Christian theology and philosophy. His Creator (who he called the *Demiurge*) is a good but not all-powerful god. He did not create from nothing but rather moulded pre-existent chaos into an orderly cosmos. And as the universe is governed by a rational principle, Plato maintained that philosophers should study such subjects as mathematics and astronomy.

Plato's most profound contribution to Greek thought was the concept that true reality is not to be found in the visible, material world, but rather in invisible, perfect and eternal Forms or Ideas, which exist neither in space nor in time. For example, the Idea of a Cube is independent of all actual cubes.

Plato's followers

Plato's immediate successors at the Academy attempted to systematize his teachings, concentrating especially upon ethics.

But Arcesilaus, who headed the Academy from 270 to 240 BC, developed a brand of scepticism independent of the sceptic Pyrrhon. He argued that if we understand Plato correctly we should suspend judgement. Arcesilaus avoided making positive statements, and claimed that he knew nothing – not even his own ignorance.

Plato, founder of the Academy in Athens.

The 'Middle Platonists' of the first century BC to the second century AD, such as Albinus, were influenced by Aristotle's view that the Divine Mind thinks only about its own thinking, because no other object is worthy of it. The Middle Platonists saw Plato's 'Ideas' as thoughts in the Divine Mind. As the Divine Mind is beyond this universe, it is the Second Mind which forms and rules the universe.

The Divine Mind can only be described in terms of what it is *not* – since all we can say about it is inadequate. The Middle Platonist view that God is beyond words and description deeply influenced Christian thinkers such as Clement of Alexandria

The last important development of Platonism was **Neoplatonism**, a movement which incorporated ideas from Aristotle and the Stoics. Neoplatonism flourished from the third century AD until the closing of the philosophical schools by the Emperor

Justinian in 529.

Neoplatonism was founded by the brilliant **Plotinus** (AD 205–70) a Greek-speaking Egyptian. He has been called 'the greatest individual thinker between Aristotle and Descartes'. On the other hand, some writers have called his emphasis upon ecstasy 'the suicide of philosophy'.

After studying for eleven years at Alexandria under Ammonius Saccus, who also taught the Christian scholar Origen, Plotinus accompanied the Emperor Gordian III in a campaign against the Persians. In 245 he established a school in Rome, but his plan to establish a city called Platonopolis in Italy was never fulfilled. Plotinus was highly regarded for his ascetic way of life; he gave away his fortune and fasted every other day.

As Plotinus wrote nothing himself, we depend for an understanding of his thought on the collection of his lecture notes, *The Enneads*, made by his famous disciple,

This means that what we can see in the world is but a pale reflection of reality, as he explained in the famous allegory of the cave in *The Republic*. Men are like the dwellers in a cave who face inwards and see only flickering shadows on the wall rather than the light outside.

We cannot grasp these Ideas through our senses. Beautiful objects, however, may lead us on to the Idea of Beauty, and sexual love (*eros*) may lead us to divine Eros. Like Pythagoras, he assumed that souls are reincarnated; we attain to a knowledge of the Ideas by recollecting what we have seen before our present existence.

Aristotle

Aristotle: 384–322 BC

Aristotle came originally from Stagira, east of Thessalonica. As his father was a physician at the Macedonian court, Aristotle was invited to become the tutor of the young Alexander, who was later to be called 'the Great'. Aristotle, it is said, was a student but not a disciple of Plato. He disagreed with his

---

Porphyry. Plotinus' system involved a single Being, and has been called a dynamic pantheism. He pictured a trinity of realities flowing out in concentric circles from the highest Being, the nameless Good taken up in self-contemplation. From the One Good radiates the Divine Mind, who in turn produces the cosmic Soul.

The lower aspect of the Soul produces the physical world, which is imperfect because it is distant from the Good. Man has a double personality, made up of the 'other man' subject to sin and suffering, and an 'eternal soul' which cannot sin or suffer. Man must struggle to achieve direct union with the Good through an ascetic life and spiritual ecstasy. Plotinus himself four times reached that extraordinary state in which he no longer knew whether he had a body.

Porphyry (AD 233–305) originally came from Tyre. In addition to editing the works of Plotinus, he wrote *Fifteen Books against the Christians*, one of the earliest attacks on the Bible. He rejected the prophecy of Daniel and criticized inconsistencies he found in the Gospels. His work was condemned by the Christian Council of Ephesus and was burned in 448, though fragments have survived.

Iamblichus of Chalcis (AD 250–330) studied under Porphyry, and then set up his own school in Syria. He commended the use of magical rites and astrology. He was renowned in his own day and later was highly regarded by the Emperor Julian the Apostate.

Proclus of Lycia (AD 411–85) was head of the Academy. He also combined magic and mysticism with philosophy. He believed that he was the reincarnation of an earlier Neopythagorean philosopher. His multitude of commentaries on Plato and other writers had a wide influence in the Middle Ages.

Although some Neoplatonists, such as Porphyry, opposed Christianity, Neoplatonism profoundly influenced many **Christian thinkers**. Origen, who studied with Plotinus, had a concept of the Christian Trinity which strikingly resembles Plotinus' trinity of the One, the *Nous* and the Soul. When they were drawing up the Nicene Creed, the theologians rejected the Neoplatonic idea that there could be grades of deity.

Augustine (AD 354–430) credited the writings of the Platonists for liberating him from the dualist views of the Manichaeans. He found their emphasis upon the invisible world and their contempt for the physical close to the Christian outlook. He claimed that 'with a few changes in their words and opinions (they) could become Christians, as many Platonists have done in recent times.'

The mystical emphasis of Plotinus strongly influenced the development of the medieval mysticism of such thinkers as Albert the Great and Bonaventure.

teacher in almost every respect. In 335 he founded his own school, the Lyceum, near Mount Lycabettus in Athens.

Insatiably curious, Aristotle investigated every conceivable subject. In contrast to Plato he stressed observation and the drawing up of general laws from observed facts (induction). He even dissected animals, and his lecture notes include studies in zoology, anatomy and physiology. Aristotle believed that reality consists in physical items rather than invisible ideas.

He laid down rules for logical argument, such as the syllogism. He wrote on poetry, rhetoric and politics. On ethics, he held that men should strive for the 'golden mean', an ideal course of conduct between extremes. Aristotle did not believe that the individual was immortal; only the impersonal 'active intellect' survived death.

He concluded, from arguments concerning motion, that there must be an Unmoved First Cause. This Prime Mover, or God, sits on the circumference of the heavens. He is solely taken up in his own thinking, and has no knowledge of the universe below.

Avicenna: AD 980–1037

Aristotle's works were passed on to the Middle Ages by Muslim writers such as Ibn Sina who was also known as Avicenna. When they were re-translated into Latin in the twelfth century AD they made a profound impact. They have had lasting influence, particularly through Thomas Aquinas, who combined them brilliantly with Christian concepts to make a crucial contribution to Roman Catholic theology.

Aquinas: AD 1224–74

Aristotle.

Aristotle's followers

Theophrastus, 371–288 BC, from the island of Lesbos, was the immediate successor to Aristotle. A popular lecturer who had as many as 2,000 students, his main contribution was in botany. Among the 270 works which are credited to him are an examination of minerals, and a humorous description of personalities called Characters, which describes such types as 'the Flatterer', 'the Chatterer' and 'the Boor'.

Another follower of Aristotle, **Demetrius of Phalerum**, was invited by King Ptolemy I to go to Alexandria and establish the 'Museum', literally 'the palace of the Muses'. This developed into a research institute which came to include the largest library in antiquity. The wealth of the Ptolemies ensured that from this time the centre for scholarship would be Alexandria rather than Athens.

It was here that **Aristarchus of Samos** (280 BC) claimed that the universe was centred on the sun; and **Eratosthenes** (274–192 BC) measured the circumference of the earth to within 200 miles (320 km) of accuracy. **Euclid**, the tutor of Ptolemy II, compiled the standard geometry textbook.

The Sceptics

Pyrrhon: 365–275 BC

Carneades: 214–129 BC

Sextus: second or third century AD

The word 'sceptic' comes from a Greek word meaning 'to observe carefully'. But scepticism came to mean disbelief or agnosticism about the possibility of knowing.

The founder of Scepticism was Pyrrhon of Elis who travelled with Alexander the Great to India. Though he left no writings, we gather from others that he distrusted the senses. He urged his followers to live calmly and base their lives on what is probable. The Sceptics dominated the Platonic Academy in the third and second centuries BC with men such as Arcesilaus. A later head of the Academy, Carneades of Cyrene was a radical Sceptic. He denied the immortality of the gods and the certainty of knowledge. All we can perceive are apparent impressions. In 155 Carneades dazzled the Romans by his rhetoric but disturbed them with his amorality.

The last major Sceptic was Sextus Empiricus who was also a physician. We are not certain where he was born or where he taught. His works included: *Outlines of Pyrrhonism*, *Against the Dogmatists*, and *Against the Professors*. He aimed for a life of quiet and his favourite expression was, 'It makes no difference.'

The Cynics

Antisthenes: 445–365 BC

Diogenes: 403–323 BC

The Cynics, who were so-called because they lived 'a dog's life' (cynic being Greek for dog-like), claimed as their founder Antisthenes, a follower of Socrates. Antisthenes rejected Plato's doctrine of Ideas and stressed a life without any worldly comforts. Most scholars, however, doubt the tradition that he founded Cynicism.

This honour most likely belongs to the most famous Cynic of all, Diogenes of Sinope, who studied under Antisthenes. He is best remembered as the man who went with a lamp in broad daylight looking for an honest man. Diogenes defied all the conventions of his day. He lived in a large jar in Corinth, and his only possessions were a cloak, a staff and a wallet. He scandalized his contemporaries by excreting and copulating in public.

Athens seen from Mt Lycabettus. To the left is the Acropolis, the fortified hill around which the city developed.

Diogenes ridiculed the attention paid to athletics, music and mathematics. He declared, 'The love of money is the headquarters of all evils'; his motto was, 'Fear nothing, desire nothing, possess nothing.' Some people admired his fierce independence. In 336 BC Alexander the Great visited him and asked what he could do for him. 'Move away, you are blocking the sun' was Diogenes' only reply. Alexander remarked, 'If I had not been Alexander, I should like to have been Diogenes.'

Crates: 365–324 BC

Diogenes' most noted pupil was Crates of Thebes. He was called the 'door-opener' because he would enter houses uninvited to harangue people with his Cynic philosophy. He converted his sister Hipparchia to Cynicism and then married her.

The Cynic preachers spoke boldly in harangues known as *diatribes*. These sermons with ethical exhortations and illustrations may have provided models for later Christian preachers.

The Stoics

Zeno: 350–260 BC

The founder of Stoicism was Zeno, from Kition in Cyprus. He came to Athens in 314 BC shipwrecked and poor. He became intrigued with philosophy after finding Xenophon's *Life of Socrates* in a bookshop. When he asked how he could study philosophy he was told to follow Crates the Cynic, who happened to be passing by. From 304 Zeno began teaching in the Painted Porch (*Stoa Poikile*), so called because of

Left: Greek town life centred on the market-place *(agora)*, which was surrounded by an arcade. Traders, philosophers, soldiers and ordinary townspeople all gathered here. At religious festivals, processions made their way through the *agora* to the temple.

Corinth, the home of Diogenes, was a prosperous Greek city-state noted for its trade and industry. In the background is the Acro-corinth, the rock on which the temple of Aphrodite once stood.

The Greek language

The Greek which was used at the Macedonian court of Alexander the Great was classical Attic or Athenian Greek. As a result of the conquests of Alexander the use of Greek became widespread, particularly as Macedonian soldiers set up their own territories throughout the Near East.

Over the centuries this Greek became simplified in its pronunciation, grammar and vocabulary, and became known as common (*koinē*) Greek. The Old Testament was translated into *koinē* by about seventy scholars in Egypt, about 250 BC. This translation is now known as the *Septuagint* from the Greek word for seventy. The *Septuagint* included not only the Old Testament books but also the dozen or so works which make up the *Apocrypha*.

The early Christians usually quoted from the *Septuagint* when showing that Scripture had been fulfilled or the identification of Jesus as the Messiah or Christ. The Jewish rabbis commissioned another Greek translation by Aquila in about AD 130. As Aquila's translation was woodenly literal, further Greek translations of the Old Testament were made by Theodotion and by Symmachus.

The Romans were in contact with the Greek colonies in Italy and Sicily from the earliest years of the Republic. But it was particularly during their wars against Macedonia and Achaea in the second century BC that Rome was flooded with Greek prisoners of war and objects of art. As the poet Horace expressed it, 'Captive Greece took Rome captive.'

The flood of Greek culture was resisted by arch conservative Romans such as Cato the Censor (234–149 BC). But an influential group of Greek-loving Romans, including Scipio Aemilianus, fostered Greek culture and served as patrons for writers such as Polybius and Terence. It was under the influence of the superior Greek culture that the Romans developed their own literature, philosophy and art. At the end of his life even Cato tried to learn Greek.

The Roman writer and orator Cicero (106–43 BC) was as fluent in Greek as in Latin, having studied at Athens and at Rhodes. Quintilian (AD 40–118), the great authority on Roman education, held that Roman children should be taught Greek before Latin. Plutarch, who lived in the second century AD, knew little Latin, and wrote his *Parallel Lives of Geeks and Romans* in Greek, using the work of Greek historians such as Polybius. The Emperor Marcus Aurelius wrote his *Stoic Meditations* in about AD 180 in Greek. The second-century satirists Martial and Juvenal complained that Roman women even made love in Greek!

Greek and Latin served as the official languages of the Roman Empire. The Emperor Augustus' autobiographical writing, the *Res Gestae* was published in Greek and Latin at Ankara, Turkey. The Emperor Vespasian founded professorships of both Greek and Latin. Greek rather than Latin was the most widely used language in the early Roman Empire except among Italians. An analysis of nearly 500 Jewish catacomb inscriptions reveals that 74 per cent were in Greek, 24 per cent in Latin, and only 2 per cent in Hebrew or Aramaic.

Greek girls playing knucklebones. This clay model, made in the third century BC, was found at Capua in Italy.

Above: scenes from a Greek school, painted on a vase. One boy learns to play the lyre while another recites his lessons.

Below: Greek pipes. Music played an important part in Greek life.

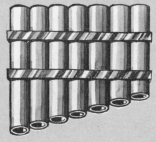

Greek was the preferred language of the early Christians. Even Christians at Rome conducted their worship in Greek until the fourth century AD. Early Christian writers such as Clement of Alexandria, Origen, Clement of Rome and Irenaeus of Lyons (in France) all wrote in Greek. With the development of 'church Latin' the Christian world eventually divided between the Latin west and the Greek east. The dividing line ran to the east of Dalmatia (Yugoslavia), Italy and Tripolitania (western Libya).

Greek education

Greek education was at first largely aristocratic and athletic, and almost always restricted to boys. After about 450 BC the Sophists, who taught rhetoric for a living, revolutionized education. In the fourth century BC great schools of philosophy were set up in Athens.

In the Hellenistic period gymnasiums were opened in every city founded by the Greeks in the Near East. These served as the main means of preserving the Hellenic tradition and of incorporating non-Hellenes into Hellenic society.

Most families would have a 'pedagogue', usually an elderly slave, who carried the boy's equipment, accompanied him to school and quizzed him on his lessons. He was a combination of 'nurse, footman, chaperon, and tutor'.

Greek educationists stressed equally athletic exercises in the nude (*gymnasia*) and the fine arts dedicated to the Muses (*mousikos*), the patron goddesses of the arts. Athletic instruction went on in private 'wrestling arenas'. Running and throwing the javelin was practised in the public gymnasiums.

Every young boy was taught to sing and to play the lyre. He would learn his ABC by copying his teacher's model letters onto his waxed tablet. He would learn to read, which in ancient times always meant reading out loud. The main works to read included Homer, lyric poetry and drama, especially the plays of Euripides.

When a boy was eighteen years old he came of age and was at last freed from the restrictive care of his pedagogue. Between the ages of eighteen and twenty Athenian youths, called *ephebes*, went through a compulsory, state-sponsored course of military and athletic training. In Hellenistic times the graduates of this training formed the upper class. In the Roman era in Athens the institution of *ephebes* formed the basis for the university there.

The Stoa of Attalus in Athens, which was built in the second century BC, has now been reconstructed.

Polygnotus' painting of the defeat of the Persians. The Stoics are named after the Stoa or colonnaded portico.

Cleanthes: ?310–232 BC

Cleanthes of Assos came from a poor family and had to work as a porter so that he could attend Zeno's lectures. He became the head of the Stoa in 262. Cleanthes saw the universe as a living being with the sun at its centre. He composed forty poems, most notably the *Hymn of Zeus*.

Chrysippus: 281–207 BC

Succeeding Cleanthes in 232 as head of the Stoa was Chrysippus, who was born in Soli just west of Tarsus, in Cilicia. He was a prolific writer, credited with over 700 works, though only fragments of these have survived. His great achievement was to systematize Stoic doctrines.

Panaetius: 185–109 BC

Panaetius of Rhodes travelled to Rome and secured as his patron the Roman general, Scipio Aemilianus, who loved Greek culture. He expounded Stoicism in such a way as to provide the Romans with a defence of their imperialism. He held that the state was more important than the individual, and that the Roman state possessed the best possible constitution. In 129 Panaetius became the head of the Stoa.

Posidonius: 135–51 BC

His student, Posidonius of Apamea established a famous school in Rhodes, where Cicero studied. The Emperor Pompey admired him, and he in turn praised Pompey and upheld Rome as a guardian of law and order. Posidonius travelled widely and wrote descriptions of various tribes, presenting the Celts in an idealistic light as 'noble savages'. A man of encyclopaedic interests, like Aristotle, Posidonius investigated mathematics, geometry, meteorology and astronomy. He noted, for example, the relationship between the phases of the moon and the tides.

Roman Stoics

Seneca of Cordoba (4 BC–AD 65) was the son of a professor of rhetoric. He served as the tutor of the Emperor Nero, and together with Burrus, commander of the praetorian guard, was responsible for the first five 'golden' years of Nero's reign.

Seneca's high position was an uncomfortable one for a Stoic philosopher. It called for compromises and made it impossible for him to live up to his high ethical ideals. He spoke of the ideal of poverty yet he was himself a millionaire. Seneca apologized by remarking: 'I am not perfect, nor ever will be. I am deep in all sorts of vices. I hope only to be better than the wicked, and to improve daily.' Of him Thomas Carlyle wrote, 'Notable Seneca so wistfully desirous to stand well with Truth and yet not ill with Nero, is and remains only our perhaps niceliest proportioned half-and-half, the plausiblest Plausible on record.'

Seneca left many moral writings and letters. He wrote nine tragedies, following Greek models, which were designed for recitation rather than for performance. His writings have been admired by such diverse figures as Queen Elizabeth I, Louis XIV, Napoleon, Shakespeare and Milton.

More admirable in his life-style was the crippled former slave, **Epictetus of Hierapolis**, in Phrygia (AD 50–138). He served as a slave under Nero's bodyguard,

Seneca, Nero's tutor.

Epaphroditus. After gaining his freedom he became a Stoic philosopher. When the Emperor Domitian expelled philosophers from Rome in about AD 90 he established a school at Nicopolis, in Epirus (Albania). Among his hearers was the future emperor, Hadrian. Epictetus left nothing in writing, but his teachings were recorded by his student Arrian in the *Diatribai* 'Lectures', and an *Encheiridion* 'Manual'.

Epictetus influenced the Emperor **Marcus Aurelius** (AD 121–80), who recorded his famous Stoic *Meditations* while campaigning against the invading Marcomanni peoples in Austria. He wrote to himself: 'Begin the morning by saying to yourself, I shall meet with the busybody, the ungrateful, arrogant, deceitful, envious, unsocial . . . I cannot be injured by any of them, for no one can fix on me what is ugly, nor can I be angry with my kinsman, nor hate him.' In spite of such lofty sentiments as 'We must love one another from the heart', and 'It is more wretched to harm than to be harmed', this Stoic emperor had little patience with Christians, who were persecuted in his reign.

A statue of the emperor and philosopher Marcus Aurelius, whose *Meditations* are still highly regarded.

The harbour at Rethymnon, the third largest town on the island of Crete. Cretans were scorned by Greek poets.

Paul and the Stoics

Tarsus in Cilicia, the apostle Paul's birthplace, was noted for such Stoic philosophers as Antipater and Zeno. Paul did not attend any 'university' at Tarsus, but left to study with Rabbi Gamaliel in Jerusalem at a relatively early age, perhaps about twelve.

Paul received only an elementary education in Greek; there are only a few quotations from the classical authors in his speeches and writings. By contrast the Christian writer Clement of Alexandria, who received an advanced Greek education, quoted Homer thirty-three times and Euripides nine times in his *Exhortation to the Greeks*.

Only three definite quotations from the classics occur in the New Testament. Writing to the Corinthians, Paul quotes from Menander's *Thais*, 'Bad companions ruin good character.' Menander wrote about a hundred plays in the so-called New Comedy style, which involved stereotyped characters in romantic plots. Paul need not have attended the theatre, however, since such quotations would be as common knowledge as Shakespeare's 'To be or not to be'.

In his letter to Titus, Paul prepared his helper to face the difficult Cretans by quoting a famous riddle from one of their own poems, Epimenides' *De Oraculis*: 'Cretans are always liars, wicked beasts, and lazy gluttons.' The original context of the quotation is: 'They fashioned thy tomb, O thou greatest and

1 Corinthians: 15:33
Menander: 342–292 BC

Titus 1:12

most high, the Cretans, always liars, vicious brutes, and lazy gluttons. But thou didst not die, but livest and art established for ever.' The Cretans held that Zeus was both born and died in their Dictaean Cave. The riddle of the poem lay in the fact that the author who said the Cretans were liars was himself a Cretan. Therefore he must be a liar, and what he said must be false; this would mean that Cretans were not liars!

Acts 17: 16-34

When Paul went to Athens he preached to the Court of the Areopagus. The Areopagus (Mars Hill) was a low hill below the Acropolis, which served as the site of the supreme court in classical Athens. By Paul's day the Areopagus Court met in the Royal Stoa – where Socrates was tried. Excavators have recently investigated this area, just north of the Athens–Piraeus railway line.

In any event there were both Stoics and Epicureans in Paul's audience. In his address, Paul quotes the phrase, 'We are also his children,' which is probably taken from the *Phaenomena* of Aratus, a poet who lived in Cilicia about 270 BC. (The phrase also appears in the *Hymn of Zeus* by Cleanthes.) Paul's remark in the first part of this verse, 'For in him we live, and move, and exist' echoes a line also found in Cleanthes, and in the same poem of Epimenides quoted to Titus, which continues, 'in thee we too live and move and exist.'

2 Corinthians 9:8
1 Timothy 6:6

Paul also uses the Stoic word *autarkeia* on two occasions, but not in the Stoic sense of an independent self-sufficiency. Rather, he re-interprets the word to mean a contentment with God's sufficiency.

When Paul was arrested in Corinth he was brought to trial before the governor, Gallio, who was Seneca's brother. A stone inscription found at Delphi refers to Gallio and dates from AD 52; it therefore enables Paul's stay in Corinth to be

Stoic teachings

Stoics were pantheists; they taught that the universe was permeated and governed by a god who created everything out of his own being, an 'intelligent fiery breath' or, as one modern writer has described it, 'a perfectly good and wise gas'. Though the Stoic god was basically impersonal, writers such as Cleanthes and Epictetus addressed him as 'Zeus'. Stoicism was able to take in all manner of popular religious and astrological notions, by interpreting them as allegories.

The Stoics believed that man himself, and especially his mind, was divine. Marcus Aurelius was determined to find happiness by worshipping the spirit in his own breast. The Stoic aimed to live in harmony with the universe, by conforming his will to Providence. He strove to achieve self-sufficiency – also a favourite concept of the Cynics – and to avoid passion.

According to Epictetus: 'It is better to die of hunger, and so to be released from grief and fear, than to live in plenty with perturbation; and it is better for your son to be glad than for you to be unhappy.' 'If you are kissing your child or wife, say that it is a human being whom you are kissing; if the wife or child dies, you will not be concerned.'

The Stoics looked upon suicide as the highest proof of human freedom. They were either agnostic or indifferent about whether man is immortal. They believed the soul is destined to be reabsorbed into the world soul at the end of the world.

dated fairly accurately. Paul could in theory have met Seneca himself, but we have no evidence for such an encounter. By the third century, however, a series of letters claiming to be between Seneca and Paul were circulating. These were accepted as genuine by the Christian leader Jerome who called the Stoic philosopher 'our own Seneca'.

Jerome: AD 348–420

Epicureans

Epicurus: 341–270 BC

Democritus: 460–370 BC

Among those that were present when Paul spoke in Athens were the Epicureans, representing the other major Hellenistic philosophy. In 310 Epicurus of Samos established a sanatorium at Mytilene, on the island of Lesbos, for those suffering from nervous disorders or depression. In 306 he came to Athens and set up a community, which included women and slaves, in a garden setting.

Epicurus took up the ideas of Democritus of Abdera who held that the world and everything in it was made up of the chance combinations of tiny indivisible atoms. Though gods may exist they are far away and have no interest in human affairs. We must therefore rid ourselves of all superstitions and the fear of death.

Epicurus, who suffered from illnesses of the stomach and kidneys, taught that man should pursue sweetness and tranquility. True happiness consists in a life free from pain, lived in quiet obscurity, surrounded by friends. Epicurus himself was far from being a hedonist who lived for the pleasures of the flesh. He remarked that 'the pleasures of sex never profited a man and he is lucky if they do him no harm.'

When his teachings reached Rome, however, the Senate banned two Epicurean philosophers in 173 BC for teaching people to pursue 'pleasures'. In the first century BC Epicurean ideas were expressed in the brilliant poem 'On the Nature of Things' by Lucretius (98–55 BC). He wrote:

The soul, no less, is shed abroad and dies
   More quickly far, more quickly is dissolved
Back to its primal bodies, when withdrawn
   From out man's members it has gone away.

The Epicureans did not believe in immortality. They would have considered the idea of a resurrection ridiculous. At death, they believed, the atoms which make up a person merely disintegrate to reform again. An Epicurean epitaph reads: 'I was not, I was, I am not, I do not care.' Crude Epicureans drew the logical conclusion, expressed in another epitaph: 'Eat, drink, play, come hither.' This is close to the phrase quoted by Paul, 'Let us eat and drink, for tomorrow we die'.

1 Corinthians 15: 32

Epicurean teachings were completely unacceptable to Christians. Jerome claimed that Lucretius suffered from fits of madness induced by drinking a love potion. Epicurean thinking passed quietly from the scene between the second and fourth centuries AD.

Near Eastern religions

The Roman writer Juvenal complained, 'Into the River Tiber pours the silt and mud of the River Orontes, bringing its babble and brawl, its dissonant harps and its timbrels'. All kinds of tributaries from the Near East were pouring their contents into the mainstream of Roman life. The Near Eastern mystery religions, with their colourful rites and promise of personal immortality, had a great appeal for the Romans.

The Sibyls
According to Roman legend, the Sibyl of Cumae, near Naples, prophesied the future to the hero Aeneas, the ancestor of the Romans. Her prophecies, recorded in the *Libri Fatales*, were supposed to have been known to Tarquin the Proud, the last Etruscan king before the founding of the Roman Republic in 509 BC.

The original Sibyl, a priestess of Apollo and of Hecate, came from either Marpessos or Erythrae in western Turkey. She was brought to Cumae, one of the earliest Greek colonies in Italy, set up in 725 BC. Her successors lived in a grotto cut 400 feet (122 m) into the rock face. The Sibyl would fall into a trance and utter her oracles in gibberish, which was then translated into metrical poetry. The oracles were written down and

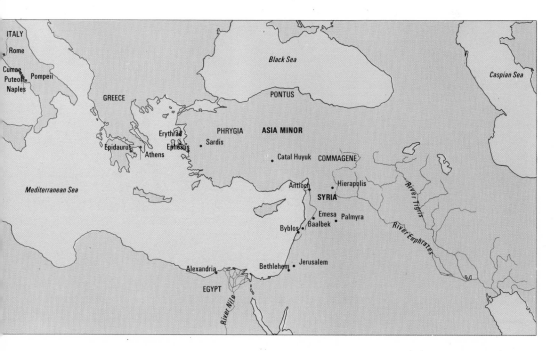

transferred to Rome, where they were looked after by a college of priests. Copies were preserved until AD 400.

The oracles put the stamp of approval on the identification of the Greek gods with their Italian counterparts, and in introducing Near Eastern gods. In 496 BC the Greek goddess Demeter and her daughter Persephone were identified with the Italian Ceres and Libera. In 293 BC, during a plague, the oracles recommended the importing of the Greek healing god Asklepios (Roman, Aesculapius) from Epidauros to Rome.

The 'Great Mother'

When Hannibal invaded Italy, the Romans found themselves in desperate straits, as their own armies proved to be no match for the Carthaginians. The Sibylline Oracles recommended introducing the cult of Cybele, the 'Great Mother' from Asia Minor. In 204 BC her cult object, a black meteorite stone, was given a temple on the Palatine Hill within the sacred boundary of the city of Rome. Foreign gods were usually kept outside this boundary.

Cybele, who is usually depicted on a throne flanked by

Cybele, the 'Great Mother' of the gods.

The goddess Diana.

lions, is a very ancient goddess; a statue of her dating from 7000 BC was discovered at Catal Huyuk. According to the Latin poet Ovid, Cybele fell in love with a young shepherd, Attis. When Attis proved unfaithful and became infatuated with a nymph, Cybele killed her. The distraught Attis then castrated himself. For this reason the priests of the cult of Cybele and Attis (the Galli) also castrated themselves. Romans were not allowed to join the cult until 102 BC, but after the Emperor Claudius had legalized it, the chief priest of the cult was an uncastrated Roman.

A gory ritual was used in this cult and in Mithraism. In the initiation rite the person would stand in a pit while a bull was slaughtered over him, drenching him in a shower of warm blood. Sometimes a ram would be used in place of a bull.

The festivities of the cult, the *Megalensia*, were held in the spring. They included a procession of Galli, whipping themselves to the accompaniment of drums and cymbals, as they mourned the death of Attis. In the second century AD the idea of a resurrection was introduced into the cult of Attis, perhaps as a result of the impact of Christianity.

Artemis of Ephesus

The temple of Artemis (Diana) at Ephesus counted as one of the Seven Wonders of the World. Artemis of Ephesus was a fertility goddess of Asia Minor, with little in common with the Artemis of Greece, a virgin huntress. Statues of Artemis of Ephesus have rows of bulbous objects on her chest, often thought to be breasts. It is more probable that they are ostrich eggs, symbols of fertility.

Acts 19: 21-41

The apostle Paul's preaching at Ephesus greatly upset the silversmiths who made a living by manufacturing statues of the goddess. A mob of 25,000 infuriated Ephesians crowded into the theatre, shouting 'Great is Artemis of Ephesus' at the top of their voices for two hours. On another occasion forty-five inhabitants of Sardis were accused of maltreating ambassadors bringing cloaks for Artemis, and were condemned to death for their crime.

Isis and Serapis

The Roman historian Plutarch tells that in ancient Egyptian myths the god Osiris was killed by his brother Seth, who trapped him in a box which was then cast into the sea. Isis, his wife, succeeded in finding his body at Byblos (Lebanon) and brought him back to life. Seth then cut Osiris into fourteen pieces. Isis once again revived him, after which he became the king of the dead.

Ptolemy I: 323–285 BC

To unite his subjects King Ptolemy I created a hybrid Egyptian-Greek god, Serapis, to serve as a new partner for Isis. He was depicted with a face similar to that of Zeus. It was Isis, however, who became extraordinarily popular in the Greek and Roman world. By 150 BC the cult of Isis was one of

Isis and Serapis with the three-headed dog Cerberus, the guardian of Hades, between them.

the most popular in Athens, as reflected by the many people named *Isidore* 'The Gift of Isis'.

By 105 BC the cult of Isis had been introduced into Italy, at Puteoli and Pompeii. The Senate attempted to banish the Egyptian cult between 58 and 48 BC and Augustus tried to do the same later. In AD 19 a Roman disguised himself as the god Anubis and seduced a woman in the temple of Isis. As punishment the Emperor Tiberius had the image of Isis hurled into the River Tiber and her priests crucified.

Caligula: AD 12–41   Caligula favoured the cult of Isis. In his reign a large temple to Isis and Serapis was built on the Campus Martius in Rome. The Emperors Domitian and Commodus similarly honoured the goddess.

Isis, who was called Panthea, was credited with the qualities of all other deities in hymns sung in her praise: 'I am the queen of rivers and winds and sea. I am the queen of war; I am the queen of the thunderbolt.' As the queen of the seas she presided over the rites which signalled the opening of the season for sailing on 5 March. Apuleius' tale, *The*

About AD 150   *Metamorphoses* or *The Golden Ass*, illustrates the importance of the cult of Isis. Lucius, the hero of the story, is turned into an ass by magic, and is made human again by the mercies of Isis.

The Egyptian rituals were exotic and colourful. The processions included shaven priests dressed in white linen and priestesses with rattles. The Roman writer Juvenal mocked the Egyptian worship of animal-gods: 'Here the highest of praise is due to the dog-headed god, Anubis, who with his linen-dressed, bald-headed throng of attendants runs along and laughs at the grief of the people.'

The gods of Phoenicia and Syria

According to Greek myth Adonis, the handsome young man loved by Aphrodite, was gored to death by a boar. It was believed that each year his blood reddened the River Afqa, near Byblos (Lebanon). Women clothed in garments of Aphrodite sowed 'gardens of Adonis' – plants which quickly sprouted and died – to commemorate the death of Adonis. Hadrian consecrated to the cult of Adonis-Tammuz the cave in Bethlehem where tradition places Jesus' birth. The idea that Adonis rose from the dead did not develop until the second century AD.

The foremost Syrian goddess was Atargatis, of the city of Hierapolis (Bambyce) on the River Euphrates. She was sometimes depicted as a mermaid, with a fish's body. Her partner was the Syrian storm-god Hadad.

Her priests, like the priests of Attis, were castrated. They were notorious beggars, who whipped themselves to attract attention and alms. The cult of Atargatis was spread to Greece (and eventually to Rome) by slaves, merchants and soldiers in the Hellenistic period (third-second centuries BC). The historian Suetonius relates that Nero despised all rites except those of the Syrian goddess, Atargatis. The Emperor Alexander Severus (AD 222–35) built her a temple in Rome.

Aphrodite was the goddess of love, beauty and fertility. This statue of her was found in Cyprus and dates from the second century BC.

Part of the colonnaded street which crossed the city of Palmyra in the third century AD.

One of the most popular Syrian gods was Jupiter Dolichenus, the god of the city of Doliche, in Commagene (between the north Syrian coast and the River Euphrates). The god was depicted standing on a bull, and holding the symbols of thunder and lightning. His cult spread during the second and third centuries AD, especially by means of soldiers. Jupiter Dolichenus was worshipped in a large temple on the Aventine Hill in Rome.

Another important god was Jupiter Heliopolitanus of Baalbek, in the Beqa'a Valley of Lebanon. A great complex of buildings still remains there, a witness to the genius of Roman architects. They were built by the Emperors Antoninus Pius, Septimius Severus and Caracalla. The huge temple of Jupiter Heliopolitanus, 106 metres long, was the largest temple with Corinthian columns ever built. Six of its original 20-metre columns still stand. The smaller temple of Bacchus at Baalbek is one of the best preserved of all Roman temples.

Less known in the west were the triple gods – Malakbel, Aglibol and Yarhibol – from the famous oasis city of Palmyra (the biblical Tadmor). Palmyra reached its highest point under Queen Zenobia, who dared to challenge the authority of Emperor Aurelian in AD 271, and it contains some of the most extensive and impressive Roman ruins in the Near East. The magnificent temple of the triple gods at Palmyra stands in a vast colonnaded courtyard, 225 metres long.

Julia Domna, the wife of the Emperor Septimius Severus, was the daughter of the high priest of the sun god of Emesa (Homs) in Syria. Her grand-nephew, Elagabalus, became emperor as a fourteen-year-old boy. He was an effeminate hedonist, who dressed in female clothes, walked on roses, and

Elagabalus: AD 218–22

feasted on ostrich brains. Elagabalus promoted the sun god of his hometown, Emesa, as the supreme god of the Empire, a project which enjoyed little popularity.

Aurelian: AD 270–75

The Emperor Aurelian defeated Queen Zenobia and reintroduced the Emesan god as 'the unconquerable sun', building him a magnificent temple in Rome. The birthday of the god, who was also identified with Mithras, was celebrated near the shortest day, winter solstice, on 25 December. The birthday of Jesus, which had been observed on 6 January by some churches, was moved to 25 December by the western churches in the fourth century AD. Augustine urged Christians to celebrate not the sun but him who made it.

Mithras

The Persian god Mithras was important in the Zoroastrian sacred writings, and also appears in the Indian Vedic writings. Worship of Mithras spread to Asia Minor following the Persian conquests of Cyrus in 546 BC. The kingdoms of Pontus and of Commagene (in modern Turkey) were ruled in the Hellenistic period by kings bearing the name Mithradates, 'The gift of Mithras'. The idea that the Persian cult developed directly into the Roman mysteries of Mithras through the activity of the magi has little support.

The earliest contact between the Romans and worshippers of Mithras resulted from Pompey's conquest of the Cilician

A bull being sacrificed by the god Mithras.

pirates in 67–65 BC. Many scholars have assumed that this marked the introduction of Mithraism to Rome, but the actual evidence points to a much later date. No Mithraic monuments were discovered either at Herculaneum or Pompeii. The writer Statius (AD 80) refers to the typical bull-slaying central to the mysteries of Mithras.

From AD 140 the cult of Mithras was spread rapidly and widely, especially by soldiers in the Danube provinces, in Germany, and as far as Britain. The cave-like sanctuaries (mithraeums) usually had a statue depicting the slaying of a bull by Mithras. Worshippers believed that this act somehow released a life-giving force. Otherwise we are still in the dark about many aspects of this mystery religion as very little written evidence has survived. Other scenes in the mithraeums picture the god being born out of a rock. Mithras is usually accompanied by two figures who represent the rising and the setting sun, Cautes and Cautopates. Initiates to the cult, who were all males, progressed through seven grades, corresponding with the seven planets then known (including the sun and the moon).

By the third century Mithraism had become one of the most potent rivals of Christianity, though it is an exaggeration to claim that the Empire would have become Mithraist if it had not become Christian. In some places, such as at San Clemente and Santa Prisca in Rome, mithraeums and churches stood side by side. Archaeologists have recently discovered a mithraeum at Caesarea in Palestine, probably dating from the reign of the Emperor Julian (AD 361–63), who favoured the cult.

Egyptian astrology

The Hermetica are an important collection of astrological and theosophical writings from Egypt. They are supposed to be by Hermes Trismegistos, the Greek title of Thoth, the Egyptian god of wisdom. The 'vulgar' Hermetica are about astrology, magic and alchemy, some of them possibly written as early as the third century BC.

The more significant 'learned' Hermetica were written in the second and third centuries AD. They are religious and philosophical, and markedly influenced by Platonism and Stoicism. They have survived in Greek, Latin and Coptic manuscripts. One of these, the myth of *Kore Kosmou*, describes how men's souls were imprisoned in bodies until liberated by Isis and Osiris.

Some of the writings hold that a single invisible God may be discerned in the heavenly order. Others declare that God gave birth to a Second Mind, the *Demiurgus* who made the planets, and also to the 'Man' who united with Nature to produce mankind. Man is therefore a dual being; his body imprisons his soul and subjects it to astrological Fate. But man may be reborn by receiving intelligence (*nous*) and suppressing his bodily senses; an initiate may at death ascend to join the heavenly gods.

Coptic texts recently discovered at Nag Hammadi in Egypt refer to the communal brotherhood of Hermetic saints who have broken the bonds of Fate, their acts of kissing, and of eating holy and 'bloodless' food.

Though some of the Hermetic writings are almost Gnostic, in Hermeticism creation is not itself regarded as evil; and the demiurge is not a rebel but the son of the supreme God.

Gnostics The Gnostics were followers of a variety of religious movements in the early Christian centuries which stressed that people could be saved through a secret knowledge or *gnōsis* (the Greek word for knowledge). The clearest evidence for these movements, known as Gnosticism, comes in Christian writings of the second century. They viewed the various Gnostic groups as heretical perversions of Christianity.

Modern scholars regard Gnosticism as a religious movement which may have been more independent of Christianity, but do not agree as to how it originated. German scholars, who define Gnosticism rather loosely, find traces of it wherever there is an emphasis upon 'knowledge' for salvation, as in the Dead Sea Scrolls. Other scholars, who define it more strictly, look for an emphasis on opposition between the pure spiritual world and the evil material world (a basic tenet of Gnosticism) before agreeing that a document is Gnostic. They believe that this 'dualistic' view of the universe is fundamental to Gnosticism.

Until the nineteenth century knowledge of the Gnostics relied entirely upon the writings of Christian leaders such as Justin Martyr, Irenaeus, Hippolytus, Origen, Tertullian and Epiphanius. Some of them preserved extracts from original Gnostic documents, but most of their accounts are in the form of counter-arguments. Scholars were thus not sure how accurate these accounts were. Recent discoveries, such as the texts found at Nag Hammadi, have confirmed some of what the early Christian writers had to say about the Gnostics. Early Christian writers regarded Simon Magus, who tried to buy the miracle-working power of the Holy Spirit from Peter and John, as the fount of all heresies. But in Acts he is not described as a Gnostic but as a *magos* or magician. Unlike the later Gnostics, Simon claimed to be divine, and taught that salvation involved knowing him rather than knowing one's self. He even had the audacity to proclaim a prostitute as the reincarnation of Helen of Troy.

Acts 8: 9-24

Simon was followed by a fellow Samaritan, Menander, who taught at Antioch in Syria towards the end of the first century. He told his followers that those who believed in him would not die. Needless to say, his own death demonstrated that he was a false prophet.

Also teaching in Antioch, at the beginning of the second

century, was Saturninus, who believed that Christ was the redeemer. But like other Gnostics he held that Christ was not a material being and only appeared to be a man.

Cerinthus taught in Asia Minor. Irenaeus even tells a story that the apostle John fled from a bath-house at Ephesus when he learned that Cerinthus was there. Cerinthus taught that Jesus was merely a man upon whom the Christ descended as a dove. As Christ could not suffer, he departed from Jesus before the crucifixion. (This tradition is also found in the Islamic Qu'ran: 'They slew him not nor crucified, but it appeared so unto them.')

Marcion of Pontus was an important, though not typical, Gnostic; he taught at Rome from AD 137 to 144. He insisted upon faith in Christ, but rejected the humanity of Jesus and the resurrection of the body.

Other Gnostic teachers included Basilides and his son Isidore, and Carpocrates and his son Epiphanes – all of whom taught at Alexandria, in Egypt. The most famous Gnostic teacher was Valentinus, who taught at Alexandria and who came to Rome in AD 140. He had a number of able followers, among them Theodotus in the east, and Ptolemy and Heracleon in the west. Heracleon's commentary on the Gospel of John is the earliest known commentary on a New Testament book.

The teachings of the Gnostics

In Gnostic beliefs there is a sharp dualism. They contrast a transcendent God with an ignorant demiurge or creator (who is often a caricature of the Old Testament Jehovah). Some taught that the creation of the world resulted from the fall of *Sophia* (Greek for 'Wisdom'). All Gnostics viewed the material creation as evil. Sparks of divinity, however, have been encapsuled in the bodies of certain 'spiritual' individuals destined for salvation.

These 'spirituals' are ignorant of their heavenly origins. God sends down to them a redeemer who brings them salvation in the form of secret knowledge (*gnosis*). Awakened in this way, the 'spirituals' escape from the prison of their bodies at death, and cross the planetary spheres of hostile demons to be reunited with God.

Since they believed that salvation depended solely upon knowing their 'spiritual' nature, some Gnostics indulged in extremely abandoned behaviour. They claimed that they were 'pearls' who could not be stained by any external mud. Carpocrates, for example, urged his followers to sin, and his son Epiphanes taught that promiscuity was God's law. The Cainites perversely honoured Cain and other villains of the Old Testament, and the Ophites venerated the serpent for bringing 'knowledge' to Adam and Eve.

Most Gnostics, however, had a harshly negative attitude towards sex and marriage. The creation of woman was the source of evil; begetting children simply multiplied the souls in bondage to the powers of darkness.

In spite of the lack of clear and early evidence, some scholars have assumed that Gnosticism has pre-Christian origins. They believe that they can detect both direct and indirect references to Gnosticism in the New Testament, especially in the writings of John and of Paul. But many of these passages can be interpreted in a non-Gnostic sense. The safest conclusion would be that an early form of Gnosticism existed at the end of the first century AD. It is altogether hazardous to read back the fully developed Gnosticism of the second century into earlier texts.

THE ROMAN EMPIRE

The Plebs, Cicero, Pompey, Caesar, Augustus, Marcus Aurelius, Constantine: the history of both the Roman Republic and the later Empire is full of famous names. For almost 1,000 years, from the birth of the Republic in 509 BC to the sack of Rome by the Visigoths in AD 410, Roman culture dominated Europe and the Near East. Latin, ancestor of several European languages including French, Spanish and Italian, remained the international language of diplomacy until the eighteenth century, and is still used today for scientific classification.

But the cultural conquest was not won without bitterness and bloodshed. The history of Rome was not always as noble as its buildings and philosophies.

The growth of the Empire

Rome's beginnings

According to the legend retold by the Roman historian Livy, Rome was founded by twins named Romulus and Remus. The Romans counted their years 'from the founding of the city' (in Latin *AUC*, for *ab urbe condita*), which corresponds to 753 BC. Archaeologists have discovered evidence which confirms this traditional date for Rome's foundation. They have uncovered crude huts on Rome's Palatine Hill as well as burials and cremations in the Forum area from this time.

Virgil's epic poem *Aeneid* traced the ancestors of Romulus and Remus back to Aeneas, the hero of Troy. This legend was current in Italy at least as early as the fifth century BC, and terracotta statues of Aeneas, carrying his crippled father Anchises, have been discovered from that period. However, in history rather than legend, Rome's early links with Asia Minor may lie in the origins of the mysterious Etruscans. These people flourished in the area north of Rome and provided the last kings of Rome in the sixth century BC.

Before the Republic was set up, Rome was ruled by Etruscan kings. This model from the fourth century BC shows an Etruscan peasant and his wife ploughing with oxen.

The Etruscans were skilful metalworkers. This gold clasp was made by an Etruscan craftsman about 650 BC.

The Roman Republic

In 509 BC the last Etruscan king was expelled from Rome. A Republic was set up, a form of government which lasted until 27 BC. In the Republic various assemblies of citizens voted in blocks to select magistrates. But Rome was not a democracy where individual citizens were free to propose and debate bills in their assemblies. Real power lay in the hands of a very few, led by the *consuls*, the two chief magistrates elected annually.

During the earliest centuries of the Republic the aristocratic Patrician class and the mass of mixed Plebeians were struggling with each other. The Plebeians tried to gain concessions by threatening to secede and create a state within the state. In 494 BC the Plebeians were given their own officials, known as *tribunes*. These were immune from arrest (they were 'sacrosanct'), and had the power of the *veto* (Latin for 'I forbid') over actions of the Senate. Their number was gradually increased from two to ten, but they were not very effective because they had to vote unanimously to uphold a veto.

In 449 BC the Law of the Twelve Tables, which every Roman boy memorized, was drawn up and published. Although only stating general rules, this marked the beginning of the great legal tradition of the Romans which was later amplified by case

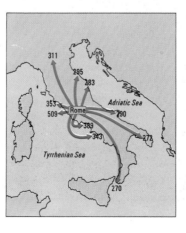

Extent of Roman territory in 201 BC
44 BC
AD 14
AD 138

The Roman Empire

law as well as statutes. In 445 a law was passed which permitted intermarriage between the Patrician and the Plebeian classes; this eventually led to the practical disappearance of any distinction between them.

Rome expands

During the fourth and third centuries BC the Romans gradually expanded their territories to include all of Italy. They first turned against their prosperous Etruscan neighbours to the north, and captured the nearby city of Veii after a ten-year siege in 396 BC. The Romans suffered a temporary set-back after the sack of Rome by the Celts in 390, but next overcame their one-time Latin allies to the south. In a series of bitter wars in the third century BC they defeated the hardy Samnites of the Apennine mountains in southern Italy, and then conquered the Umbrians to the north.

The Romans gave many of their defeated foes Latin rights. These gave them the private privileges of citizenship, including the rights of marriage and trade. Defensive colonies of Roman citizens were established on the various frontiers of the Italian territories.

Roman conquests

Threatened by Roman expansion, the Greek city of Tarentum in southern Italy invited Pyrrhus, a cousin of Alexander the Great, to fight against the Romans. He met their request with his army of 20,000 men and twenty elephants. Though he won victories between 280 and 275 BC, Pyrrhus suffered such casualties that he said, 'another victory like this and I am lost', a statement from which we derive the expression 'a Pyrrhic victory'.

The versatile Romans improved their military tactics with each encounter with a new enemy. By the third century BC they were ready to launch wars of aggression, though they claimed they were for defensive reasons.

In the First Punic War against the Phoenician colony of Carthage in Tunisia, North Africa, the Romans made up for

Originally a Phoenician port, by the fifth century BC Carthage was capital of a large empire. When the Romans captured it in 146 BC they razed the city to the ground. These remains date from Roman times.

their lack of a navy by quickly building copies of a captured Punic ship. They invented the grapnel, a rod with a spike which could be used to immobilize enemy ships before boarding. Their victories gained the Romans their first overseas territories – the islands of Sicily, Corsica and Sardinia.

Rankled by this humiliating defeat and by the heavy war-payments imposed by Rome, Hannibal launched the Second Punic War by attacking from Spain and crossing the Alps into north Italy with his troops and elephants. Hannibal defeated the Romans at the River Trebia, Lake Trasimene and Cannae, trapping the legions with his clever tactics and outflanking them with his superior Numidian cavalry. Though he was not able to capture the city of Rome or dislodge her Italian allies, he was virtually unmolested as he tramped up and down the Italian peninsula for a dozen years. But the Roman general Scipio Africanus finally drew Hannibal away by threatening Carthage itself; he defeated him at Zama in 202.

The Third Punic War was demanded by the magistrate (*censor*) Cato who ended every speech he made in the Senate with the cry 'Carthage must be destroyed'. In due course Scipio Aemilianus destroyed the city, sowing salt over its fields to destroy the crops.

After the Romans had defeated Hannibal they turned to deal with King Philip V of Macedon who had allied himself with **200–196, 171–167 BC** Carthage. In a series of Macedonian Wars the small fighting units of 100–200 men of the Roman legions proved too mobile for the solid but inflexible Macedonian fighting units, called phalanxes. A further Greek revolt – by the Achaean League – resulted in 146 BC in the devastation of the city of Corinth, which did not rise from its ashes for a century.

The Macedonian campaigns brought Rome enormous treasures and a flood of slaves. In contrast the war against the **143–133 BC** stubborn city of Numantia in Spain brought nothing but hardship. Soldiers returning home found that their families had been forced to sell their farms to survive during their long absence.

This distressing situation prompted the Gracchi brothers to attempt reforms between 133–123 BC. They wanted to see public land redistributed. But the wealthy aristocrats (*Optimates*) were not prepared to grant any concessions to the people's party (*Populares*). They reacted by first killing Tiberius Gracchus in 133 BC, and then his brother Gaius Gracchus in 123 BC.

The bitter hostilities between these two parties erupted in a violent civil war between the followers of the *Populares*, led by Marius, and the *Optimates*, led by Sulla. Marius was a war **Jugurtha: 112–106 BC** hero who had defeated the Numidian leader Jugurtha and who had saved Rome from invading Germanic hordes in 102 and 101 BC. Though he was a 'new man', the first member of an

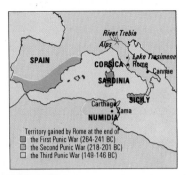

The Punic Wars

Left: a Punic well and grave at Utica in Tunisia – one of many cities which fell to the Romans at the end of the Third Punic War.

Right: part of the Roman road, the Appian Way, which was the scene of mass executions after Spartacus's unsuccessful revolt.

obscure family to achieve a state office, he was repeatedly elected consul. This highest office ordinarily went only to members of the twenty-five noble families who could number consuls among their ancestors.

Sulla was appointed general in 88 BC to deal with Mithradates, an ambitious king of Pontus, northern Turkey. Mithradates had launched a crusade against the grasping Roman businessmen and tax collectors who had invaded Asia Minor after the last king of Pergamum bequeathed his kingdom to the Romans in 133. Mithradates ordered the slaughter of 80,000 Romans in a single day, and had molten gold poured down the throat of one Roman official. Though forced to accept terms by Sulla, Mithradates was to prove a persistent foe.

Internal unrest

The last century of the Republic was marked by inter-factional violence. Roman generals, following the example of Sulla who first marched his army against Rome, used their own followers to try to enforce their policies.

90–88 BC

Unrest among the Italians led to the Social War. This finally resulted in the granting of citizenship to almost all Rome's Italian allies. Unrest among the gladiators and slaves led to the

73–71 BC

famous revolt led by the gladiator Spartacus, whose motley mob defeated several Roman armies. When the Roman leaders Crassus and Pompey finally crushed the revolt they crucified 6,000 rebels along the Appian Way, outside Rome.

As the Romans' destroyed the navy of Rhodes, pirate raids in the Mediterranean became so frequent that they threatened

Roman trade and the vital grain supplies. Even Caesar himself was once captured by pirates and held for ransom. To suppress them Pompey was given unlimited powers for three years. He in fact accomplished his task in three months, and went on to subjugate much of Asia Minor and make Palestine a Roman province.

67–63 BC

Cicero, though a 'new man', achieved election as a consul in 63 BC by his brilliance as an orator and writer. He enjoyed his finest hour in denouncing the conspiracy of Catiline, but spoilt his reputation by constantly reminding his readers of his achievement.

Frustrated by conservatism in the Senate, three ambitious politicians formed the secret agreement known as the 'First Triumvirate' in 60 BC. The three men were Pompey, Caesar and Crassus. Crassus, the wealthiest individual of his day and seeking military glory, led an ill-fated expedition against the Parthians. At Carrhae (called Harran of the book of Genesis) in 53 BC Crassus' army was surrounded by Parthians who shot an unceasing shower of arrows upon his ranks. The Romans suffered one of their costliest defeats ever, losing 20,000 men.

Left: Julius Caesar, the general who became dictator of Rome.

Right: Mark Antony, co-ruler of the Empire after Caesar had been murdered.

Julius Caesar

After his year as consul, Caesar left Rome to serve as the proconsul or governor of Gaul (France). There, between 58 and 51 BC, he defeated innumerable Celtic and Belgic armies, massacring hundreds of thousands in the process. He twice invaded Britain, though it was not made a province until the later invasion of the Emperor Claudius in AD 43.

When Pompey persuaded the Senate to order Caesar to lay down his arms at the end of his period as proconsul, Caesar challenged them by crossing the River Rubicon in 49 BC. As this marked the boundary between his province of Cisalpine Gaul and Italy, the die was cast for war. In the civil war which followed, Pompey's followers outnumbered Caesar's. But in 48, on the plains of Pharsalus in northern Greece, Caesar decisively defeated Pompey. Hoping to find refuge in Egypt, Pompey fled to Alexandria but was murdered as he landed.

Caesar travelled to Egypt in pursuit of his enemy, and there became infatuated with Queen Cleopatra, the last of the Ptolemaic rulers of Egypt. After extricating himself from a difficult military position in Alexandria with the aid of the Jews, Caesar proceeded to mop up pockets of opposition with rapidity. He had great plans and reforms in mind: he revised the calendar (his 'Julian' calendar, with minor changes introduced by Pope Gregory, is the one we use today), and planned a colony for Corinth. But because he arrogantly took up the powers of dictator, some of his close friends, including Brutus, joined in a plot to assassinate him in 44 BC, on the Ides of March, the 15th.

In a speech immortalized in drama by Shakespeare – 'Friends, Romans, countrymen' – Mark Antony aroused the people to a fever pitch against the assassins who found it prudent to leave the country. Much to his own chagrin Antony found that Caesar's will did not name him heir; instead Caesar's young grandnephew, Octavian, was nominated successor. After some bitter feuding, Antony and Octavian, together with Lepidus, formed a Second Triumvirate in 43 BC to pursue Caesar's murderers. One of their first acts was to sentence to death the orator Cicero, who had bitterly attacked Antony in a series of speeches.

The crucial battle was fought at Philippi, Macedonia, in 42. Brutus and Cassius, the leaders of the assassins, were disheartened, partly because of faulty communications, and committed suicide.

The victors divided the Empire: Octavian was to rule the west and Antony the east. Antony summoned Cleopatra to appear before him at Tarsus. He was captivated by her, though he was married to Octavian's sister, the noble Octavia. Egged on by the ambitious queen, Antony eventually divorced Octavia and proclaimed Caesarion, Cleopatra's son, the legitimate heir of Caesar.

But outside the bay of Actium in north-western Greece, Antony's fleet was outmanoeuvred by Octavian's admiral, Agrippa in 31 BC. Instead of attempting to rally his dispirited troops, Antony shamelessly joined Cleopatra in flight. After a half-hearted attempt to defend Egypt, he committed suicide. Cleopatra clasped a poisonous asp to her breast, and was buried at Antony's side in Alexandria.

Leaders of the Empire

Augustus: 27 BC–AD 14

In 27 BC Octavian was granted the title Augustus and became the first 'emperor', a term which is derived from the military title *imperator*. Technically he was no more than first senator. But as he combined in himself all the powers of consul, tribune and other offices, he had no rival. Augustus shrewdly kept direct control of all the military provinces which held the major part of the armed forces. He wisely avoided Caesar's mistake, by behaving deferentially to senators. In his reign Roman peace (*Pax Romana*) was extended as far as the Danube and the Black Sea.

Augustus, the first Roman emperor.

Augustus was not only the first emperor, he was also the greatest. He justly deserved the title 'father of his country'. He passed many wise and far-sighted measures concerning both Rome and the provinces. He boasted that he had transformed Rome from a city of brick into a city of marble.

His genuine piety, celebrated in the famous Altar of Peace in Rome, led to his restoring eighty temples. Augustus also attempted to regulate morals, and banished his own daughter Julia for her immorality. He tried to use legislation to encourage marriages and births, and his censuses do indicate an increase in the number of citizens from 4,233,000 in 8 BC to 4,937,000 in AD 14. It was during an era of peace in his reign Luke 2: 1 that Jesus was born in Bethlehem rather than at his parents' home in Nazareth because a census ordered by Augustus required all adults to register at their ancestral home towns.

Tiberius, emperor at the time of Jesus' crucifixion.

Tiberius: AD 14–37   The Emperor Tiberius was the son of Livia, the empress, by a previous marriage. Though an able soldier, his dour personality did not impress Augustus. For his part Tiberius resented the shabby manner in which he was treated, in particular by being forced to divorce his beloved Vipsania to marry Augustus' adulterous daughter Julia.

Tiberius' reign was marred by a glut of treason trials. In AD 26, at the age of 67, he was persuaded by Sejanus, the sinister chief of the praetorian guard, to retire to his luxurious villa on the island of Capri, near the bay of Naples. According to the scandalous stories repeated by the writer Suetonius, the emperor indulged himself with orgies and sadistic displays, and rarely ventured back to mainland Italy. In AD 31 the treachery of Sejanus was uncovered and he was summarily executed. In either AD 30 or 33, Jesus was crucified under Sejanus' protégé, Pontius Pilate, prefect of Judea – a fact which was known to the Roman historian, Tacitus.

Luke 23: 24-25

Gaius: AD 37–41

The Emperor Gaius was nicknamed Caligula, 'Baby-boots', by the troops of his father, the popular Germanicus. At first he seemed to be a good emperor, but he soon revealed himself as the most depraved monster to occupy the imperial throne. Utterly immoral, he committed incest with his sisters, humiliated senators and acted with calculated cruelty. A megalomaniac who claimed to be divine, Gaius threatened to set up a statue of himself in the Jewish temple in Jerusalem. He was assassinated in his palace in AD 41.

Claudius: AD 41–54

Claudius, Gaius' uncle, was a scholar who, because of his physical deformities, was not taken very seriously before his accession as Emperor. A victim of infantile paralysis (polio), he stumbled as he walked, stuttered as he spoke, and even slobbered at the mouth. He surprised everyone by becoming a conscientious emperor. He added no less than five provinces to the Empire, including Britain and Mauretania (Morocco). To run the bureaucracy Claudius appointed his freedmen, including Pallas, to such posts as the treasury. The apostle Paul, who conducted most of his missionary activities during the reign of Claudius, languished for two years in prison at Caesarea when Felix, brother of Pallas, was procurator of Judea.

Acts 24: 26

Claudius was unwise in his choice of wives, however. His first wife, Messalina, was so brazenly unfaithful that the emperor was persuaded to have her executed. Like some absent-minded professor, Claudius would sometimes forget she had been executed and wonder why she was not present at dinner. His next wife, the ambitious Agrippina, murdered him by feeding him poisoned mushrooms so that her son, Nero, could succeed to the throne.

Nero: AD 54–68

Nero was the last of the Julio-Claudian line of emperors. After five 'golden years' under the guidance of Seneca and Burrus, Nero decided to rule himself. He first got rid of his domineering mother, after several bungled attempts which included a collapsing ceiling and a disintegrating ship.

Though Roman writers are unanimous in blaming Nero for the great fire which devastated Rome in 64, this is not very likely. Fires were all too frequent as many of Rome's buildings were firetraps. To divert blame from himself Nero made scapegoats of the Christians and had them executed in his gardens – the area where the Vatican now stands. Paul and

Below: the Emperor Claudius, who made Britain a Roman province.

Right: Nero, the first emperor to persecute the Christians.

Below: the Emperor Claudius, who made Britain a Roman province.

Right: Nero, the first emperor to persecute the Christians.

Peter were probably martyred at Rome in the persecutions which followed.

Nero did not exactly 'fiddle' while Rome burned; he is said to have played a lyre. He seriously fancied himself a musician and inflicted his talents on captive audiences. Hired crowds provided him with unfailing applause. An admirer of Greek culture, he went to Greece to participate in the Panhellenic games. Needless to say, he was awarded the first prize in all events – even when he fell off a chariot. He proudly displayed all the gold crowns he won in his magnificent Golden House which he had erected after the great fire. Nearby he constructed a gilded-bronze statue of himself as Apollo 30 metres/33 yards high.

As various plots were made against him, Nero panicked. He ordered men such as Seneca and Gallio to commit suicide. When the end came, his bodyguards deserted him, and with a servant's help he, too, committed suicide lamenting, 'What a great artist perishes.' Nero's place was taken in the year 69 by a rapid succession of emperors – Galba, Otho and Vitellius.

Above: Vespasian, the son of a tax-collector, rose to power in the army.

Right: the Forum at Pompeii with Mt Vesuvius in the background.

The Flavian emperors

Vespasian: AD 69–79

Titus: AD 79–81

Domitian: AD 81–96

Revelation: 1:9

Nerva: AD 96–98

Vespasian was the first of the Flavian line of emperors. He had served ably as a general in Britain and in Judea, and left his son Titus to finish the operations against the Jews. His major task as emperor was to restore the finances which Nero had so prodigally squandered. He succeeded by making economies with such extreme measures as a tax on the public urinals.

Titus was universally popular for his generosity. His brief reign was marked by another fire in Rome, a plague, and most notably the unexpected eruption of Mount Vesuvius in 79. The volcano buried the town of Herculaneum in a tidal wave of mud and Pompeii in a shower of ash and pumice. An eyewitness account of the eruption has been preserved in the letters of Pliny the Younger.

The younger brother of Titus, Domitian, resented the way his father and his brother had kept him in the background. When he became emperor he ruled as a despot. He demanded that he be addressed as 'Lord and God', and persecuted Jews and Christians. It was in his reign that John wrote the Revelation, as a prisoner on the island of Patmos. Domitian's reign of terror was cut short by his assassination.

The next emperor, Nerva, was an elderly senator who served primarily as a caretaker-emperor, thus avoiding the chaos of AD 69. He chose as his successor a capable Spaniard, Trajan.

Emperors from abroad

Trajan: AD 98–117

Trajan was the first provincial leader to become emperor. In a series of military campaigns (101–6) he conquered Dacia north of the Danube (modern Rumania), a feat which he commemorated in spiral relief on a column in Rome (now topped with a statue of the apostle Peter). He also annexed the kingdom of the Nabataeans as the province of Arabia (Transjordan and the Sinai peninsula), and temporarily wrested Armenia and Mesopotamia from the Parthians.

How the Romans viewed the Christians

Pliny's letter to Trajan:
It is my custom, lord emperor, to refer to you all questions whereof I am in doubt. Who can better guide me when I am at a stand, or enlighten me if I am in ignorance? In investigations of Christians I have never taken part; hence I do not know what is the crime usually punished or investigated, or what allowances are made. So I have had no little uncertainty whether there is any distinction of age, or whether the very weakest offenders are treated exactly like the stronger; whether pardon is given to those who repent, or whether a man who has once been a Christian gains nothing by having ceased to be such; whether punishment attaches to the mere name apart from secret crimes, or to the secret crimes connected with the name.

Meantime this is the course I have taken with those who were accused before me as Christians. I asked them whether they were Christians,

and if they confessed, I asked them a second and third time with threats of punishment. If they kept to it, I ordered them for execution; for I held no question that whatever it was that they admitted, in any case obstinacy and unbending perversity deserve to be punished. There were others of the like insanity; but as these were Roman citizens, I noted them down to be sent to Rome.

Before long, as is often the case, the mere fact that the charge was taken notice of made it commoner, and several distinct cases arose. An unsigned paper was presented, which gave the names of many. As for those who said that they neither were nor ever had been Christians, I thought it right to let them go, since they recited a prayer to the gods at my dictation, made supplication with incense and wine to your statue, which I had ordered to be brought into court for the purpose together with images of the gods, and moreover cursed Christ – things which (so it is said) those who are really Christians cannot be made to do. Others who were named by the informer said that they were Christians and then denied it, explaining that they had been, but had ceased to be such, some three years ago, some a good many years, and a few even twenty.

All these too worshipped your statue and the images of the gods, and cursed Christ.

They maintained, however, that the amount of their fault or error had been this, that it was their habit on a fixed day to assemble before daylight and recite by turns a form of words to Christ as a god; and that they bound themselves with an oath, not for any crime, but not to commit theft or robbery or adultery, not to break their word, and not to deny a deposit when demanded.

Trajan's reply to Pliny:
You have adopted the proper course, my dear Secundus, in your examination of the cases of those who were accused to you as Christians, for indeed nothing can be laid down as a general ruling involving something like a set form of procedure. They are not to be sought out; but if they are accused and convicted, they must be punished – yet on this condition, that whoso denies himself to be a Christian, and makes the fact plain by his action, that is, by worshipping our gods, shall obtain pardon on his repentance, however suspicious his past conduct may be. Papers, however, which are presented unsigned ought not to be admitted in any charge, for they are a very bad example and unworthy of our time.

This correspondence between the Emperor Trajan and Pliny, governor of Bithynia, shows how Christianity had spread, and how it was treated, in the second century AD.

Left: a section of Trajan's column erected in the Roman Forum in AD 113 to commemorate his victories over the Dacians. Scenes from the wars were carved in a continuous spiral on the column.

Right: the Emperor Hadrian (AD 117–38) reduced the size of the Empire and fortified its boundaries.

Another Spaniard and a relative of Trajan, Hadrian, was noted as an admirer of Greek culture, a perpetual traveller, and a prodigious builder. On becoming emperor, he wisely abandoned the newly conquered territories of Armenia and Mesopotamia and drew the eastern border of the Empire at the River Euphrates. In the west Hadrian built the famous wall named after him between England and Scotland. He rebuilt Agrippa's Pantheon in Rome, and erected a sumptuous villa at Tibur (Tivoli). The great circular mausoleum where he was buried is known today as the Castel San Angelo. During his reign the second great Jewish War of Bar Cochba broke out (131–35).

Antoninus: AD 138–61

Marcus Aurelius: AD 161–80

His successor, Antoninus, was the first emperor from Gaul. He was so noted for his integrity, scrupulousness and gentleness that he was called Pius. His successor, Marcus Aurelius, is best known for his Stoic philosophy and his *Meditations*. His reign was beset with plagues and with invasions along the Danube frontier, and he died on a campaign at Vienna.

Commodus: AD 180–92

His unworthy son, Commodus, was as ignoble as his father was noble. More concerned with gladiatorial games and races than government, Commodus was a complete disgrace. He was assassinated by the imperial guards (*praetorians*), who promptly auctioned off the throne to the highest bidder.

The Severi

Septimius Severus: AD 193–211

After the brief reigns of Pertinax and Didius Julianus in 193, a new line of six rulers called the Severi came to power. The first of these was Septimius Severus, who had been born in Leptis Magna in Libya. This city was lavishly beautified by the

Severi; its ruins today are among the most extensive and
magnificent in the world.

Caracalla: AD 211–17   Severus' advice to his son Caracalla 'Enrich the soldiers and
scorn all other men', was followed. In order to raise taxes and
recruits for the army, Caracalla granted citizenship to all free
men in the empire in 212. But by this time Roman citizenship
had become more of a burden than a privilege.

Elagabalus: AD 218–22   Elagabalus introduced the sun god of his native town of
Emesa in Syria as the supreme god of the Empire. He was
despised for his decadence and licentiousness and was killed
by the praetorian guard. His successor, Severus Alexander
(222–35) was born at Acre in Palestine. He worshipped equally
Abraham, Jesus and Apollonius of Tyana. The Empire was at
this time threatened by the new Sassanian Empire in Persia in
the east, and by barbarians on the German frontier. Once
more the emperor was killed by rebellious soldiers.

Septimius Severus, who spent much of his
reign on military campaigns, first in
Parthia and then in Britain where he died.

Christianity and emperors

During the next fifty years (235–85) no less than twenty-six
emperors of barrack-room origins reigned in rapid
succession; only one of them died a natural death. Among

Decius: AD 249–51   them was Decius who launched an Empire-wide persecution
of Christians.

Diocletian: AD 285–305   Diocletian, who was from Illyricum (Yugoslavia), also began
a savage persecution against Christians. He attempted to
improve the deteriorating economy by fixing prices. The
measure backfired as merchants withheld their goods from
sale or resorted to barter. Inflation was rampant. Within forty
years a peck of wheat costing 100 denarii had risen to 10,000
denarii under Diocletian.

Diocletian attempted to rule the Empire with a system of four rulers (tetrarchy): an Augustus and a Caesar in the west and an Augustus and a Caesar in the east. The Caesar of the west was Constantius Chlorus, the father of Constantine. When Diocletian abdicated in 305, open war broke out in the attempt to decide upon his successor.

Constantine claimed to have received a vision that he should conquer in the sign of the *Chi-Rho* (the first two Greek letters in the name of Christ). In 312 he defeated the Emperor Maxentius at the battle of the Milvian Bridge, north of Rome. In 313, together with Licinius, Augustus of the west, Constantine issued the Edict of Milan granting toleration to all religions, including Christians.

Constantine served as sole emperor from 324 to 337 and openly favoured Christianity, though he himself was not baptized until shortly before his death. In 325 he called the Council of Nicaea, an important gathering of Christians to discuss matters of doctrine, and in 330 he established the new capital of Constantinople at Byzantium. His mother, Helena, built the Church of the Holy Nativity over the grotto in Bethlehem which was the traditional birthplace of Christ, and the Church of the Holy Sepulchre over the traditional site of Calvary.

Above: the Emperor Constantine.

Below: Portchester Castle in Hampshire, England, was built by the Romans about AD 300 to defend the coast against Anglo-Saxon invaders.

Organizing the Empire

Roman government

Rome acquired many overseas provinces in the period of the Republic. It became customary for ex-magistrates, known as 'proconsuls', to be sent to them to act as governors. In the early Empire there were two types of province: relatively pacified areas were known as 'senatorial' provinces, and were ruled by proconsuls; the restless frontier provinces were governed by imperial legates. By the second century AD the emperor governed both types of province. A special case was the wealthy province of Egypt, which no senator could visit without the emperor's permission.

Few governors were as just and as fair-minded as Cicero, governor of Cilicia in 51 BC. More were like the notorious Verres, governor of Sicily, whom Cicero prosecuted for extortion. Provincials could do little to complain about a governor's conduct while he was in office; he could only be tried after his period in office expired. Of Albinus, governor of Judea from AD 62 to 64, Josephus wrote: 'Not only did he, in his official capacity, steal and plunder private property and burden the whole nation with extraordinary taxes, but he accepted ransoms from their relatives on behalf of those who had been imprisoned for robbery by the local councils.' (The Acts 24: 26 writer of Acts suggested that the governor Felix hoped for a bribe from his prisoner, the apostle Paul.)

A particularly galling aspect of the governor's powers was his authority to billet troops and to requisition transport or other services. It was this practice which Jesus referred to Matthew 5: 41 when he said 'And if one of the occupation troops forces you to carry his pack one mile, carry it two miles.' It was also by using Matthew 27: 32 this authority that the Romans forced a passer-by, Simon of Cyrene, to carry Jesus' cross.

As the governor normally resided in the capital and made only periodic circuits through his province, the normal day-to-day government would be left in the hands of local officials. These were members of the aristocratic class who had the leisure to take part in municipal politics, and the wealth to pay for the services that were expected of them. Erastus of Romans 16: 23 Corinth, who was converted to Christianity by the apostle Paul, was the treasurer of the city. A Latin inscription from ancient Corinth names an Erastus who is the commissioner of public works (*aedile*) and may refer to the same individual.

Other municipal officials named by Luke in the book of Acts Acts 17:6 include the *politarchs* of Thessalonica, and the *asiarchs* of

Acts 19:31   Ephesus who tried to dissuade Paul from going to the theatre where a riot was in progress. The *asiarchs* were drawn from the wealthiest men of the province. The town clerk
Acts 19:35   (*grammateus*) of Ephesus was no mere figurehead but the democratic city's executive officer.

Roman taxes

The Romans and those in the provinces had to pay all kinds of taxes. There were direct taxes on land and other personal property, known as *tributum*, and a variety of indirect taxes, the *vectigalia*. In Judea during Caesar's day $12\frac{1}{2}$ per cent of the harvest was due as a tax. Every adult, including women and slaves, had to pay a poll tax of about a denarius – a day's wage. (Denarius was translated 'penny' in the King James Version of the Bible; and the symbol for the old British penny was *d* for denarius.) There was a general sales tax of 1 per cent and an inheritance tax of 5 per cent. People who bought slaves were charged 4 per cent of their cost, and 5 per cent if they freed one.

An important source of revenue was the customs dues collected on both exports and imports at harbours and selected frontier posts. Some scholars believe that Matthew,
Matthew 9:9   who worked as a tax collector at Capernaum and Zacchaeus
Luke 19:2   who was the chief 'tax collector' at Jericho, a frontier post between Judea and Perea, were toll collectors. The toll on goods was usually between 2 and $2\frac{1}{2}$ per cent, except on the luxury perfumes from Arabia which were taxed at 25 per cent.

Towards the end of the Roman Republic taxes were collected by tax-farmers called publicans drawn from the equestrian class. They would submit tenders for the contract to collect taxes in a province, pay the sum tendered in advance, and then try to collect as much as they could over and above that as profit. Such a system led to rapacity and abuse, and was replaced after the Emperor Trajan by officials who received a fixed percentage of the taxes as income. The publicans in Judea were assumed to be dishonest, a fact which can be verified from both rabbinical documents and the New
Luke 19:8   Testament. (Zacchaeus, for example, said to Jesus 'if I have cheated anyone, I will pay back four times as much'.)

In the last years of the Empire, as emperors tried to raise funds to support both their ostentatious luxury and the army, they bled their peoples white with taxation.

The Roman army

The Roman army included three categories of soldiers: the praetorian guard, the legionaries and the auxiliaries.

Praetorian guard
The praetorian guard was the emperor's bodyguard, formed by Augustus. It consisted of between twelve and sixteen cohorts, each of about 500 men, stationed at Rome. The praetorians enjoyed the highest pay, had the shortest term of service – sixteen years – and the lightest duties. During his

imprisonment in Rome the apostle Paul was chained to a member of the praetorian guard (Acts 28: 16, 20). As a result of his preaching the Christian message spread throughout the praetorian camp. The Emperor Claudius set a precedent by awarding the praetorians a pay-bonus upon his accession; from his time the guards played a key role in setting up a new emperor when the previous one had been assassinated.

Legionaries

The major armed forces were the infantry, or legionaries, who were recruited from among Roman citizens. By Trajan's time Italy itself provided only one out of every five legionaries. The normal age for enlistment was nineteen, though some started serving as early as fourteen. A minimum height of 4 feet 11 inches (1·48m) was expected; this was raised in AD 367 to 5 feet 5 inches (1·64m).

During the reign of Augustus there were twenty-five legions. This total was raised to thirty-three under Septimius Severus. Ideally each legion had ten cohorts of 540 men each, or 5,400 men all told. Because of casualties, legions were more often than not under strength. Each cohort was further subdivided into six centuries of ninety men, commanded by a centurion. Attached to each legion would be a wing of 120 cavalry.

The New Testament speaks of a man who said that his name was 'Legion' because so many demons had possessed him (Mark 5:9). When he was arrested Jesus declared that if he wished he could call upon more than twelve legions of angels to assist him (Matthew 26:53).

Legion officers

The chief officer of a legion would be a legate of senatorial rank. He would be assisted by a staff of six military tribunes of either senatorial or equestrian rank. During the period of the Roman Republic every aspiring politician was expected to serve in the army for about ten years before he ran for election.

As officers were chosen by reason of social rank and not military experience, many were poor soldiers. In AD 9 a commander named Varus allowed himself to be led into the Teutoberg Forest in Germany, where he was ambushed and lost all his men. Augustus would cry out in the middle of the night: 'Varus, Varus, give me back my three legions!'

Centurions

The backbone of the army were the centurions, who were veteran soldiers. When the centurion was promoted he was usually transferred to another legion to prevent him from getting too friendly with the men under his command. The centurions were paid about

Below: a soldier from the praetorian guard armed with a sword, shield and javelin.

Below right: a centurion carrying a short vinewood staff as a symbol of rank.

The Roman army attacks an enemy town.
The siege has been carefully planned.
A wall and ditch have been built around the
town so that none of the defenders can
escape or reinforcements attack the
besieging army. Now the assault begins.
   Catapults hurl boulders at the enemy
forces on the walls. Further down, a giant
wooden tower has been pushed up a
specially-built ramp, close to the walls.
Soldiers on the top of the tower fire arrows
at the enemy. Close by, other soldiers use
ladders to scale the walls. A battering-ram
is being used to break down the main gate.
Behind it a small detachment, with their
shields locked together in a 'testude' or
'tortoise', prepare to rush in. In the
foreground legionaries wait to follow up
the attack.

fifteen times as much as the ordinary soldier, or about 5,000 denarii per year (in Trajan's reign). The five senior centurions received 10,000 denarii, and the first javelin or chief centurion of the legion received 20,000 denarii.

Pay and equipment

The ordinary legionary received between 225 and 300 denarii per

An auxiliary protected by mail armour, brandishing a long sword.

year as wages, out of which he had to pay for his food and clothing. He would also be supplied a 'salt ration' (*salarium* – from which we get our word 'salary'). His diet would consist of bread, grain in the form of porridge, and the kind of sour wine offered to Jesus on the cross (Matthew 27:48).

Each legionary soldier carried a pack weighing about 80 pounds (36 kilos). This included about two weeks' rations, and tools such as spades and axes. He wore a helmet of bronze reinforced with iron over a leather skull cap. He had a segmented breastplate made of metal plates and leather, and a belt. On his feet he wore thick-soled sandals with hobnails. For protection he carried a shield of laminated wood bound in metal and covered with leather. The offensive weapons he used were two 7-foot javelins, but he relied mainly on his 2-foot long sword. Though it was two-edged, it was usually employed to stab rather than to cut and thrust.

Paul used the imagery of such a soldier's armour in his letter to the Ephesians: 'Stand ready, with truth as a belt tight round your waist, with righteousness as your breastplate, and as your shoes the readiness to announce the Good News of peace. At all times carry faith as a shield; for with it you will be able to put out all the burning arrows shot by the Evil One. And accept salvation as a helmet, and the word of God as the sword which the Spirit gives you.'

Rights and privileges

After twenty years of service the legionaries would be discharged and granted land in a frontier colony such as Carthage, Corinth or Philippi. In England such colonies were established at York, Lincoln, Colchester and Gloucester. (The ending 'chester' or 'cester' derives from the Latin *castrum* meaning 'camp'.)

Until the edict of Emperor Septimius Severus in AD 197 all soldiers up to the grade of centurion were forbidden to marry. Married men who joined the service had to dissolve their marriages. But excavations and inscriptions from military camps reveal that many women did accompany the soldiers. Some of these were called 'wives' though in law they were concubines. On being discharged, a soldier received a small bronze folded certificate (*diploma*), granting him the right to contract marriage and bestowing citizenship on his descendants.

After AD 140, however, because of the shortage of recruits, citizenship was granted to the sons of veterans only if they enlisted in the army. By the end of the second century most new recruits were the offspring of soldiers and their concubines.

Auxiliary troops

In addition to the legionary forces there were equal numbers of auxiliary troops drawn from non-citizens. After twenty-five years of service these men received citizenship. Many of the auxiliaries were experts with special weapons, such as the archers from Syria and the slingers from the Balearic Islands off the east coast of Spain. They were recruited primarily from the border provinces, and in the early years of the Empire served near their homes.

The soldiers of Judea in the first century AD were mainly auxiliaries recruited from the Gentile populations of Sebaste (Samaria) and Caesarea, and had little sympathy for the Jews. In the story of Cornelius in Acts chapter ten a cohort of Italian volunteers is mentioned, which was attached to the auxiliary forces in Judea. Cornelius, a centurion of this band, may have been a local volunteer (despite his Latin name) as his family is mentioned.

The people of Rome

Senators At the highest level of Roman society were members of the Senate, the important advisory council which in the Republic controlled finance, foreign policy and military operations. Its 600 members were each expected to have a minimum of a million sesterces, roughly the equivalent of £30,000. As the law excluded them from trading by sea and through state contracts, they invested their wealth in large estates. Senators wore tunics with broad purple stripes.

With the growth of the Empire the Senate declined in importance. Many senators were killed, suspected of challenging the emperors. Between the reigns of Nero and Nerva (about AD 88–96) half of the old senatorial families were eliminated. During the Empire the emperor's cabinet of between twenty and thirty personal associates known as the 'friends of Caesar' became more important than the Senate.

Equestrians The Roman 'knights' (*equites*) were originally the 1,800 cavalry of the Republican army, whose horses were supplied by the state. By 400 BC wealthy men who could provide their own horses also became equestrians. As the army relied

Cicero, the orator, warning the Senate of a plot to seize power.

increasingly on the auxiliary forces for its cavalry, the equestrians became a political order rather than a military division.

The number of senators was limited, but the number of equestrians was not. By 225 BC 21,000 qualified for membership of this class. In the theatre the orchestra seats were reserved for senators while the first fourteen rows of seats behind the orchestra were reserved for equestrians.

Towards the end of the Republic equestrians acted as businessmen and as publicans collecting taxes. In 123 BC they gained the right to sit in the courts which tried extortion by provincial governors, and became a strong political force.

By the first century BC citizens could qualify as equestrians if they had a minimum of 400,000 sesterces or about £12,000. They were given the privilege of wearing a toga with a thin purple stripe, and a gold ring. Some writers have suggested that the rich man with 'gold fingers' who entered the Christian 'synagogue', mentioned in James' letter in the New Testament, may have been an equestrian.

James 2: 2

During the Empire the emperors used the equestrians to counter possible threats to them from senators. Only an equestrian could serve as governor of Egypt and head of the praetorian guard. Equestrians also served as officers in the army and as governors over 'minor' provinces such as Judea. By the time of the Emperor Diocletian most of the administrative and military offices were filled by equestrians.

The poorer classes

Long periods of service abroad were required of soldiers during the Numantine War (143–133 BC). Many farmers were dispossessed of their land after lengthy service abroad and they drifted into the city of Rome, becoming part of the urban mob. Tiberius Gracchus was moved by their plight and said: 'The wild beasts that roam Italy have their dens and lairs to shelter them, but the men who fight and die for Italy have nothing but air and light. Homeless and footless, they wander about with their wives and children . . . They are called masters of the world, they have no clod of earth to call their own.'

Tiberius Gracchus was killed in 133 BC by senators who were opposed to his proposals of land reform, as was his brother Gaius Gracchus twelve years later. However, the *lex frumentaria* which Gaius passed in 123 BC provided subsidies to sell grain at cheap prices to the free townspeople. This later developed into distribution of free grain called the 'dole'.

Roman conquests provided a massive influx of prisoners of war who provided cheap labour for the wealthy. Small farmers who could not compete sold their lands to the wealthy and swelled Rome's population. The heads of families eligible for the dole rose from 150,000 in the second century BC to 300,000, at which point Julius Caesar cut the number in half again. Augustus kept the number down to 200,000. At the very least 600,000 persons – or half the population of Rome – depended upon the dole. Only a minority of free citizens were able to earn their own living; the rest lived on 'welfare'.

Free citizens who were not members of the senatorial or the equestrian classes comprised the so-called 'third estate'. Most of them formed a lower class rather than a middle class. There was a huge gulf between the emperor, senators and wealthy freedmen with fortunes of 20 to 30 million sesterces, and those who tried to live modestly within an income of about 20,000 sesterces per year. This was the goal which the writer Juvenal set himself: 'When can I assure myself that I will preserve my last years from the beggar's staff and mat? Twenty thousand sesterces paying interest, well secured . . . that is enough for a poor man like me.'

ost of the poorer people lived in ercrowded blocks of flats without mbing or adequate heating. This is a del of such a block at Ostia.

The poor man's lot was not a very happy one. He would live in an upstairs garret with a bare minimum of furniture, and with a single short toga as protection against cold nights and days. He would drink sour wine, and eat mainly bread and vegetables; a sheep's head or a pig's head was a luxury. Worst of all was the social stigma of being poor. The writer Juvenal complained: 'If you're poor, you're a joke, on each and every occasion. What a laugh, if your cloak is dirty or torn, if your toga appears a little bit soiled, if your shoe has a crack in the leather. Or if several patches betray frequent mending! Poverty's greatest curse, much worse than actually being poor, is that it makes men objects of mirth, ridiculed, humbled, embarrassed.' In fact, the slaves of wealthy men were far better off than most free but poor Roman citizens: 'Sons of freeborn men give way to a rich man's slave.'

Wealthy Roman citizens lived in luxury villas. Murals were painted on the walls and the floors were inlaid with mosaic. A great deal is known about the style of these villas from buildings excavated in Herculaneum and Pompeii, which were preserved almost intact under a deep layer of mud and ash when Mount Vesuvius erupted in AD 79.

The main picture shows the garden-courtyard of a villa which was surrounded by a covered passage or 'peristyle'. The owner's wife is seated in a wicker chair, attended by one of her many slaves. Close by is the 'Lares', the shrine to the household gods.

The inset shows a cross-section of a typical villa. The main entrance is on the left and the room beside it was sometimes used as a shop. The central room in the villa is the 'atrium' which has a shallow pool to collect rainwater falling through a square opening in the roof. Stairs lead from the atrium to the bedrooms on the floor above. The dining-room and kitchen open on to the peristyle.

Slaves

People could become slaves because of debt, through kidnap and sale, and by being born to enslaved parents. But more than all of these sources combined was the provision of thousands of slaves from the prisoners of war.

There were very few slaves in Rome until the overseas expansion of Rome in the third century BC. By the second century BC there were estimated to be 250,000 slaves. Out of an estimated total population of 1,200,000 in Rome during Trajan's reign at the turn of the first century, one-third – about 400,000 – were slaves. After that date the number of slaves declined.

Slaves were primarily Epirotes (Albanians), Greeks, Scythians, Phrygians and Syrians. The principal slave markets were at Alexandria, Delos, Ephesus and Byzantium. The average rich citizen would own one or two slaves. But Pliny the Younger owned 500, and a wealthy man called Isidorus possessed over 4,000.

Slavery was so widespread that, apart from philosophers, few gave it much thought. Plato described the slave as 'a troublesome piece of goods'. Aristotle believed that some were by nature inferior and destined to be slaves, though he also urged humane treatment of them, but only out of calculated self-interest. The Stoics had some success in stressing that slaves were human beings, but even they did not seek to abolish slavery.

A slave was considered by Roman law to be a piece of goods. This made it possible for more than one man to share the ownership of a slave. But although a slave was a chattel, he was nonetheless a person in certain religious and social matters. A slave's oath was considered binding, his curse effective, and his grave a religious site. He could join an association of workmen (*collegium*) that held common meals and cared for the burial of its members. During Hadrian's reign a law was passed forbidding a master to kill or torture his slave.

Enlightened masters allowed slaves their own personal funds with which they could buy their freedom, sometimes in seven years. Household slaves were well-treated and were even regarded with affection. When Cicero's brother Quintus freed a favourite slave, Cicero wrote: 'I have just heard about Tiro. He ought never to have been a slave, and now you have decided that he should be our friend instead.' Luke records an incident when a centurion asked Jesus to heal his slave 'who was very dear to him'. On a number of occasions slaves are reported to have saved their masters' lives.

Luke 7:2

Among wealthy households, such as the emperor's, there was a special slave for each task. There was a slave who served as wet nurse, another as child attendant, others as midwife, nurse, secretary, clerk, reader, footman, and bedroom attendant. In the textile trade there were spinners, wool-workers, weavers, weighers, clothes-makers, menders

This mosaic of a slave dates from the third century AD.

and folders. This specialization meant that much of Roman slavery was 'neither eternal, nor, while it lasted, intolerable.'

Some slaves were given considerable responsibilities, even to the extent of owning other slaves. The politician Crassus had a slave staff of 500 architects and masons. Other slaves worked in factories making pottery and glass objects. The most oppressed slaves were those who had to work in mines; many were chained together and forced to work in cramped tunnels.

Some masters treated their slaves savagely. Seneca, who himself argued for kind treatment, described the lot of oppressed slaves: 'The poor slaves may not move their lips, even to speak. The slightest murmur is suppressed by the rod; even a chance sound, a cough, a sneeze, or a hiccup, is met with the lash. There is a terrible penalty for the slightest breach of silence. They must stand all night, hungry and dumb.'

Such treatment led to a number of spectacular slave revolts. The best known was that led by the gladiator Spartacus, who gathered a band of 70,000 rebels and fought off Roman armies between 73 and 71 BC. After defeating the pirate Sextus Pompeius in 36 BC, Octavian returned 30,000 fugitive slaves to their masters for punishment or executed them himself. During Nero's reign a harsh law was passed which prescribed death to all slaves in the household of an official murdered by one of them.

But nevertheless many slaves did run away. There was Cicero's slave, for example, who stole some of his books, and

Philemon 10-12

the slave Onesimus, who Paul befriended and sent back to Philemon. The law prescribed penalties for harbouring runaways, and if one was caught he could be crucified, or branded with an 'F' for *fugitivus*.

The emperor's own household contained an enormous number of slaves – sometimes more than 20,000. According to

Philippians 4:22

Paul's letter to the Christians at Philippi some of these and other slaves were among the first to follow Christianity. Names such as Ampliatus, Urbanus, Stachys, Tryphaena, Tryphosa and Hermes, mentioned in Romans chapter sixteen, were common slave names. Though first-century Christians did not call for the abolition of slavery, they welcomed slaves as brothers in the faith, and some of them even became leaders in the church. It was not until the eighteenth century that a Christian, William Wilberforce, pioneered the abolition of slavery in Europe.

Freedmen

An important class in Roman society were the *libertini*, freedmen or former slaves. There was a synagogue of freedmen in Jerusalem, whose members disputed with the

Acts 6:9

Christian preacher Stephen shortly before his martyrdom.

There were various reasons for freeing slaves; some were

A Roman relief showing a second-century AD draper's shop. Two rich customers, attended by their slaves, watch while the shop assistants open a box containing a pillow.

altruistic and others not. Many masters set their slaves free as reward for special services, for religious reasons, or in their wills in order to gain a posthumous reputation for magnanimity. In some cases it was cheaper, since as freedmen former slaves would be fed from the grain dole. But even after liberation freedmen owed allegiance to their masters as patrons, and their names would identify their former owner.

One extraordinary feature of the Roman political system was that with some limitations freed slaves became Roman citizens. They could not become senators, no matter how wealthy they might become; and they rarely achieved equestrian status, unless they were freed imperial slaves. Most freedmen formed a kind of lower middle class. Unlike the free but poor Roman citizens, they were not afraid to dirty their hands in making money. They were quite willing to engage in the so-called 'sordid' occupations listed by Cicero: 'fishmongers, butchers, cooks, pastry-cooks and fishermen . . . perfumers, dancers and the whole tribe of gamesters.'

Some freedmen became exceptionally wealthy; but despite their riches they were despised. The freedman Trimalchio, in Petronius' book *Satyricon*, is noted for his wealth and his boorish ostentation. Others achieved lasting fame for their literary works: Livius Andronicus was an early Latin poet; Terence, a slave from north Africa, became an outstanding writer of theatrical comedies; and Epictetus was a famous Stoic philosopher.

Christian masters often freed their slaves. Some of the earliest bishops of Rome, such as Pius (AD 140–54) and Callistus (AD 217–22) were probably former slaves.

ROMAN LIFE AND BELIEFS

Ancient Rome had all the trappings of modern city life, without its technology. People were housed in tall apartment blocks and luxurious suburban villas, which were connected to a sophisticated water supply and drainage system. There were impressive – and functional – public buildings: offices, libraries, theatres, arenas, temples and baths. And a network of roads speeded trade and communication.

As in other periods of history, material prosperity did not quench religious aspirations; it may even have fostered them. Astrology, emperor worship and a host of mystery religions were not merely private indulgences but a part of Roman public life.

Social organization

Marriage and divorce By the time of the Emperor Augustus the minimum legal age
for marriage was set at twelve for girls and fourteen for boys, a
standard which was later adopted by church canon law. The
Roman writer Plutarch explained that girls were married at a
youthful age to ensure their purity. As a girl who was still not
married at nineteen was considered an 'old maid', anxious
parents would increase her dowry and publicize this fact to
attract suitors. Augustus made inheritance and political
advancement difficult for women who were not married by the
age of twenty, and men who were not married by the age of
twenty-five.

In the early years of the Republic fathers exercised an
absolute authority over their children, whom they could sell or
even kill. Women were under a man's guardianship; they did
not even have individual names – Claudia and Julia, for
instance, are simply clan names with feminine endings. In the
later years of the Republic, however, women became more
and more liberated.

Marriages were usually preceded by a betrothal, which
could involve children as young as seven. The male placed an
iron ring on the fourth finger of his betrothed and kissed her.

The best seasons for weddings were considered to be April
or the second half of June because the omens were good. Fully
one-third of the days of the year were regarded as ill-omened,
especially the days when the spirits of the dead were thought
to be at large, during the feasts of Parentalia and Lemuria.

Before the wedding the bride would give up her toys and
her childhood dress to her household gods. She would dress
in a white tunic of flannel or muslin, and wear a bright orange
veil which left her face exposed. The ceremonies were
completed when the bride moved publicly to her new home.
The groom went ahead, scattering walnuts to children. He
would then carry his bride over the threshold to prevent her
from stumbling – which would have been unlucky.

Ordinarily second cousins could not be married. But by the
second century BC even marriage between first cousins was
tolerated. The marriage in AD 49 of the Emperor Claudius to
his niece Agrippina set a shocking precedent.

Slaves had no personal rights, so did not have the right to
contract a Roman marriage. A union involving a slave could
either be recognized or repudiated by the master. Once a
slave was freed his first act would be to buy his 'wife's'

freedom. According to laws introduced by Augustus, 'Freeborn men are forbidden to marry a prostitute, a procuress, a woman set free by a procurer or procuress, one caught in adultery, one convicted in a public action, or one who has been an actress.'

During the Republic children were welcomed and the lack of children lamented. A famous epitaph of Turia from the first century BC explains how a wife urged her husband to divorce her as she was barren so that he might take another wife.

Early in the Empire, however, there was a sharp decline in the number of children who were born and who were raised. Some women, we are told, avoided motherhood for fear of losing their beauty. Others resorted to abortions or abandoned their babies in the cess channels. Of the babies who were born more girls than boys were abandoned to die. A list of the public assistance given to illegitimate children in the time of the Emperor Trajan includes 145 boys but only thirty-four girls.

In the early history of Rome divorce was rare. But by the later years of the Republic and early period of the Empire divorces had become quite common among the upper ·classes, often for political and sometimes for completely trivial reasons. Pompey married five times, Caesar four. The writer Seneca commented: 'No woman need blush to break up her marriage since the most distinguished ladies have adopted the practice of reckoning the year not by the names of the consuls but by the names of their husbands. They divorce in order to

The *atrium* was the main living room in luxury villas such as this one in Herculaneum. A square opening in the roof let in light and rainwater which fell into a shallow pool underneath.

Ivory combs used by wealthy Roman ladies.

remarry. They marry in order to divorce.'

In the early years of the Republic a man could divorce his wife for such serious crimes as adultery, poisoning his children, or counterfeiting his keys; but a woman could not initiate a divorce. Later in the Republic, with the prevalence of 'free' marriages, a wife could start divorce proceedings. A husband who caught his wife in the act of adultery had the right to kill her and to mutilate or kill her lover. Augustus made adultery a public crime; under his law a husband still had the right to kill a man of lower class caught in adultery.

Because of the hazards of childbearing more than half of the wives died before the age of forty. On the other hand, because husbands were often about ten years older than their wives, and were exposed to the dangers of war, wives frequently outlived them.

Numerous epitaphs present a picture of marital bliss. A common phrase is that the couple lived for so many years 'without a single quarrel'. Wives were praised for being 'content to stay at home', 'modest', 'obedient', 'careful over money', and 'religious but not superstitious'.

Roman education

The Romans copied the Greeks in using pedagogues for their children, often employing Greek slaves for this purpose, but down-to-earth Romans introduced some striking differences from Greek education. Mathematics, geometry and music were taught only where they had practical applications. Rhetoric, not philosophy, was regarded as supreme among the higher studies, and the Romans disliked the nudity of Greek athletics.

Girls attended the elementary schools along with boys, in contrast to Greece where boys alone attended school. Some women were able to get such a knowledge of literature that Juvenal complained: 'How I hate them. Women who always go back to the pages of Palaemon's grammar, keeping all of the rules, and are pendants enough to be quoting verses I never heard.'

Schools were held in any available space, sometimes in open market-places. Some were held in a shed in front of a house, separated from the public by a thin partition. For their arithmetic lessons, pupils would use an abacus with pebbles.

The children attended the elementary school, which in Latin was called 'play', from the age of seven to ten or eleven. (The word school itself comes from the Greek word for 'leisure'.) Parents demanded much from the teacher but paid him little – sometimes only after a court-order. Aesop's Fables were popular for the teaching of reading.

Discipline was a vital part of education. A painting from Pompeii depicts a boy being held by two others as he is flogged on the back by a teacher. The Latin phrase meaning 'to withdraw the hand from the rod' meant to leave school. The writer Quintilian protested against the universal practice of flogging maintaining that praise, competitiveness, and even play were better incentives than fear.

From the age of twelve till fifteen or sixteen, when the young Roman came of age and donned his white *toga*, he would attend the secondary or grammar school. The main subjects taught here were technical grammar and literature, primarily Homer and other Greek writings. It was not until 25 BC that Latin works were also introduced. These included the writings of Virgil, Cicero, Terence and Horace.

After grammar school, until the age of eighteen or twenty, the young men received training in rhetoric. As Rome was transformed from a Republic into an Empire, political opportunities decreased and training in rhetoric became more and more divorced from real life. Students were asked to declaim on some action, such as 'should the mythical King

A Roman school in Gaul. Two pupils are unrolling their papyrus scrolls as a third arrives late.

Agamemnon sacrifice his daughter?' or on some far-fetched case involving a conflict of laws.

The rhetoricians taught various figures of speech. The apostle Paul uses about thirty different rhetorical figures in his writing, and may have received some elementary training in rhetoric at Tarsus. But whatever his training, Paul deliberately gave up the use of the elaborate and pompous rhetorical language so commonly used to gain applause by orators of his day.

Crime The Roman police force was manned by the fire-fighting *vigiles*. But they could do very little to prevent crime in a city with a population of about a million. There were clothes-snatchers at the baths, burglars who entered houses, and brigands who waylaid travellers. The wealthy who travelled at night employed their servants to keep criminals at bay. As Juvenal relates, it was the solitary traveller who was attacked by hoodlums:

Here is how it all starts, the fight, if you think it is fighting
When he throws all the punches, and all I do is absorb them.
He stops. He tells me to stop. I stop. I have to obey him.

What can you do when he's mad and bigger and stronger
  than you are? . . .
If you try to talk back, or sneak away without speaking,
All the same thing: you're assaulted, and then put under a
  bail bond for committing assault.
  This is a poor man's freedom.
Beaten, cut up by fists, he begs and implores his assailant,
Please, for a chance to go home with a few teeth left in his
  mouth.

Trade

With the establishment of peace within the Empire (*Pax
Romana*) under the Emperor Augustus, trade flourished
between Rome and different parts of the world, including the
Near East and the Far East.

Ancient Sheba (modern Yemen) in south-western Arabia
and ancient Punt (Somalia) in east Africa are the only places in
the world where the short trees which provide myrrh and
frankincense grow. These resins were used as perfumes,
incense for religious purposes and medicines. Myrrh, for
example, was used in Queen Esther's six-month beauty
treatment, as a pain killer and for embalming corpses.

Dyed cloth was one of many Roman imports. This modern picture shows traders selling cloth in the market at Beersheba, Israel.

These valuable substances were shipped by the Arabs and
the Nabataeans to Gaza and to Alexandria for processing. The
Roman writer Pliny the Elder reported that workmen in the
factories at Alexandria were stripped bare and thoroughly
searched for any stolen goods before they were allowed to
leave the premises.

It is estimated that fifty million sesterces a year went to
Arabia for the purchase of these incenses and other luxury
items such as corals and pearls. Pliny believed that the natives
of southern Arabia were the wealthiest race in the world.

Rome's major rival in the east was the formidable Parthian
Empire which decisively defeated Crassus in 53 BC and

Opposite: important Roman imports.

Trade with India

Horace, the Roman poet of the period of Augustus, claimed, with a poet's exaggeration, 'now the Scythians and proud Indians seek rulings' from Rome, and that the Chinese dared not break the commands of the emperor. The first ambassadors from India did come in the reign of Augustus, bringing snakes, pearls, precious stones, and a boy born without arms.

The Romans sent an expedition under Aelius Gallus to explore the Red Sea in 25 BC. The key to Rome's trade with India, the value of which grew to fifty million sesterces per year, was the discovery, possibly in the reign of Tiberius, that the monsoon winds blow from the south-west from April to October, facilitating travel to India, and from the north-east from November to March for the return trip from India to the Red Sea. When the Romans learned this, they were able to cut out the Arab middlemen.

From India came such items as parrots, tortoise shell, mother of pearl and precious jewels. Especially valued imports included plant products and spices such as ebony, nard, cassia, cinnamon and pepper. Rice was grown in India and in Syria but was not a major import to the Roman Empire; Horace referred to it once as a medicinal gruel. Cotton was grown in India, Persia and Judea.

The Roman presence in India has been confirmed by archaeological excavations. Archaeologists have discovered considerable fragments of Arretine pottery and Roman glass at Arikamedu, near Pondicherry, and Roman coins dating from the reign of Augustus at various sites.

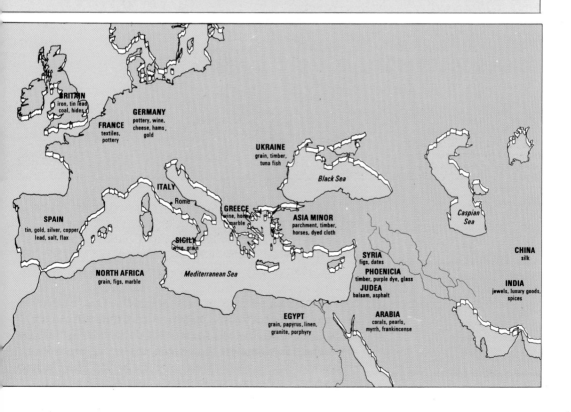

BRITAIN
iron, tin lead coal, hides

GERMANY
pottery, wine, cheese, hams, gold

FRANCE
textiles, pottery

UKRAINE
grain, timber, tuna fish

Black Sea

ITALY
Rome

SPAIN
tin, gold, silver, copper lead, salt, flax

GREECE
wine, honey, marble

ASIA MINOR
parchment, timber, horses, dyed cloth

Caspian Sea

SICILY
wine, grain

SYRIA
figs, dates

CHINA
silk

NORTH AFRICA
grain, figs, marble

Mediterranean Sea

PHOENICIA
timber, purple dye, glass

JUDEA
balsam, asphalt

INDIA
jewels, luxury goods, spices

EGYPT
grain, papyrus, linen, granite, porphyry

ARABIA
corals, pearls, myrrh, frankincense

Antony in 36 BC. In 20 BC Augustus was able through negotiations to recover the lost Roman standards captured by the Parthians. Peace with the Parthians opened up the way for trade through the vast Parthian territories.

The Emperor Augustus commissioned Isidore of Charax to explore both sides of the Persian Gulf. In his work *The Parthian Stations* Isidore described the overland routes through Mesopotamia and Persia, which eventually became the famed Silk Road to China. This route stretched for 4,000 miles from Syria through Mesopotamia and Persia up to Bactria (northern Afghanistan) and then through Turkestan to China. The first direct contact between Rome and China came about when a delegation was sent to the Han court in China in AD 160.

Silk had been manufactured in China from the third millennium BC, and was used by the Achaemenid kings of Persia during the fifth and fourth centuries BC. Silk was sent to weaving centres in Syria, Phoenicia and Galilee, where it was interwoven with linen or wool, and then dyed. Pure woven silk was not used until the Emperor Elagabalus made a robe of such material.

The overall economy of the Roman Empire was unbalanced, with massive wealth concentrated in the hands of a very few people. They spent enormous sums on imported luxury goods, and as this was sent outside the Empire, it was of no benefit to the much poorer masses.

A Roman merchant ship, used to carry cargoes of grain.

Sea travel   Sea travel depended upon the seasons. The best time to travel was the summer, between 26 May and 14 September. The winter, 10 November to 5 March, was so hazardous that only pressing circumstances such as war would make people sail. The periods in between, 14 September to 10 November and 5 March to 26 May, were risky for sailing. Paul's famous shipwreck (Acts 27: 39-44) probably took place in October.

Paul was sailing as a prisoner to Rome in an Alexandrian grain ship which carried 276 passengers. Such ships were about 180 feet/55 metres long and displaced 1,200 tons. The Jewish historian Josephus, who was also shipwrecked on his way to Rome, was travelling on a ship which carried 600 people.

Imperial couriers could ordinarily travel between Rome and Palestine within about fifty days. Merchants covering the same distance took about 100 days. The post, however, was subject to various delays. When Petronius, the legate of Syria, disobeyed Caligula's command, the emperor sent a message in December AD 40 ordering his execution. Caligula was assassinated on 24 January 41. Happily, news of the emperor's death reached Petronius in February, twenty-seven days before the first message. This all took place during the winter season when sea travel was extremely risky.

Books and libraries

In the ancient world people wrote primarily on papyrus sheets obtained from Egypt. (The English word 'paper' comes from 'papyrus'.) Since the Greeks imported their papyri through the Phoenician port of Byblos, the Greeks called a book *biblos* (from which comes the word 'Bible').

When the city of Pergamum in Asia Minor was deprived of a supply of papyri, they invented parchment – specially prepared skins of sheep and goats. Other writing materials included leather, broken potsherds (*ostraca*), and waxed tablets in school. The apostle Paul asked Timothy for the 'parchments' – probably a request for scrolls of the Old Testament.

2 Timothy 4: 13

Ancient Hebrew and Aramaic manuscripts were written without vowels, though some consonants were used to indicate long vowels. Greek texts were written without punctuation and often without gaps between words. Ancient writings such as the scriptures were often on papyrus or leather scrolls, some as long as 30 feet/9 metres. With such scrolls it was difficult to find particular passages. (The chapter and verse divisions of the Bible were introduced only in the fifteenth and sixteenth centuries AD.)

The first Christians adopted the book form (*codex*) for their scriptures for easier reference. We have fragments of twelve papyrus *codices* from Egypt dating from as early as the second century AD: seven of these are of the Old Testament, three of the New Testament. One is the so-called 'Egerton' Gospel, and the other a portion of a writing called the *Shepherd of Hermas*. Pagan writers did not adopt the *codex* widely until the third and fourth centuries AD.

The earliest known libraries were collected by Peisistratus, a ruler of Athens, and by Polycrates of Samos, both in the sixth century BC. The thinkers Plato and Aristotle collected books for their schools. The first public libraries were established by the Greeks. The library at Alexandria was the largest in the ancient world, and had between 500,000 and 700,000 scrolls with identifying tags arranged on shelves. Bucket-like containers held multiple scrolls for lengthy works, and the library's catalogue filled 120 scrolls. Another major library was at Pergamum (in modern Turkey).

The Romans acquired libraries from their wars in Macedonia and Achaea. The general Aemilius Paullus brought back the library of King Perseus, and Sulla the books of Aristotle. Cicero collected his own library, and had his slaves

The Roman language

The oldest surviving writing in Latin is on the Praeneste gold brooch, dating from the seventh century BC, and is written from right to left. The most important early inscription is the Lapis Niger from the forum in Rome, dating from the sixth century BC, and written from left to right, right to left, alternately. Latin literature only developed in the second century BC, influenced by Greek writing. Few Latin inscriptions survive from earlier than the first century BC.

The golden age of Latin literature came through the patronage of the Emperor Augustus. From his reign come the writings of the poets Virgil and Horace, the

A mosaic of Virgil writing the *Aeneid,* **attended by two Muses, patron goddesses of the arts.**

historian Livy, and the geographer Strabo. One writer, Ovid, incurred the wrath of the emperor for his writings on amorous subjects. He was exiled to the Black Sea coast of Bulgaria, the Roman equivalent of Siberia.

While Nero ruled, the Stoic philosopher Seneca was writing, as was his nephew Lucan, the author of the *Pharsalia* which is about the battle between Julius Caesar and Pompey. Petronius wrote the obscene *Satyricon,* which reveals the decadence of Nero's reign.

During the period of the Flavian emperors the encyclopedic *Natural History* of Pliny the Elder was written, together with the *Institutes* of Quintilian, on education, the technical treatises of Frontinus, the poetry of Statius, and the satires of Martial. From the reigns of Trajan and Hadrian come the letters of Pliny the Younger, the satires of Juvenal, Suetonius' *Lives of the Caesars,* and the historical works of Tacitus.

It was more common for Italians to study Greek than for people in the provinces to study Latin. But Latin was indispensable for anyone aiming at a career in law or politics. In the provinces Latin was only used for official and military documents.

The inscription on Jesus' cross was in Latin, Greek and Hebrew (or Aramaic in Hebrew letters). However, apart from numerous Latin proper names, there are only about twenty-five Latin words in the Greek New Testament. A number of these are found in the Gospel of Mark which many scholars believe was written in Rome.

An interesting Latin inscription was discovered in 1961 at the excavations of the theatre in Caesarea. It contains the first mention of Pontius Pilate in an epigraph, and refers to a temple dedicated to the worship of the Emperor Tiberius.

The first major Christian theologian to write in Latin was the fiery Tertullian of Carthage (AD 197–222), although he quoted his scriptures in Greek. However, Cyprian, bishop of Carthage (AD 200–58) quoted scriptures from a Latin translation now known as the *Old Italic* version. Above all others it was Jerome (AD 347–420) who made Latin the language of the western church. He spent thirty-five years in Bethlehem translating the Bible into Latin from the original Hebrew and Greek, and his version, the *Vulgate,* is still referred to today.

employed copying manuscripts. The Emperor Trajan established the magnificent *Bibliotheca Ulpia* with Greek and Latin works and reading rooms. Hadrian established a library in Athens, one wall of which still stands today. By the fourth century AD there were twenty-nine public libraries in Rome.

Libraries were also established by the Christian scholar Origen (185–254) at Caesarea, and by Bishop Alexander at Jerusalem before AD 212.

Medicine in the ancient world

Hippocrates of Cos (460–380 BC) was the legendary 'Father of Medicine'. However, none of the medical writings associated with his name, which date from 450 to 350 BC, can be credited definitely to him. Physicians today still swear the so-called 'Hippocratic Oath', which includes the words: 'That you will exercise your art solely for the cure of your patients, and will give no drug, perform no operation, for a criminal purpose, even if solicited, far less suggest it.'

Empedocles of Agrigentum (490–435 BC) founded a medical school which asserted that all illnesses are caused by the imbalance of four humours: blood, phlegm, yellow bile and black bile.

Herophilus of Chalcedon (early third century BC) carried out his research at Alexandria. He not only dissected corpses but even vivisected criminals. He realized that the brain was the centre of intelligence; the Egyptians had dismissed it as

The Aesclepium was a health centre founded at Pergamum by a man from the city who was cured at the shrine of Aesclepius, the god of healing, in Epidaurus, Greece. The centre included a temple, library, theatre and sleeping accommodation.
Below: the vaulted tunnel leading to the treatment room. Cold water was sometimes poured on people as they passed through it, as shock therapy. Right: a view of the Aesclepium.

mere stuffing for the head. Herophilus was able to distinguish between sensory and motor nerves, and between veins and arteries. In contrast to the Hippocratic school, which held that arteries carried air, he claimed that they transmitted blood.

Another medical scholar of third-century Alexandria was **Erasistratus of Chios**. He believed that disease was caused by over-eating and recommended dieting as a cure. He demonstrated that animals lose weight by using energy.

In the Roman Empire the outstanding medical authority was **Galen of Pergamum** (AD 130–201), who studied at Smyrna, Alexandria and Corinth. He belonged to a school known as the 'Dogmatics', because they believed that they were the only ones who had the truth. Galen served as a physician to emperors from the time of Marcus Aurelius until Septimius Severus. He was led to some mistaken conclusions because he limited his dissections to animals.

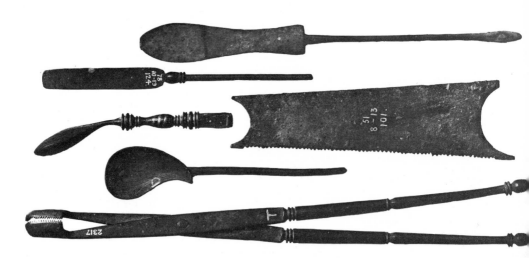

A collection of surgical instruments used by Roman doctors.

Soranus of Ephesus, who flourished in the second century AD, was the leading member of the 'Methodist' school of medicine. The Methodists recognized only three possible diseases: excessive dryness, excessive humidity, and imbalance of the humours. Soranus wrote a treatise titled *How to Recognize the Newborn Child That Is Worth Rearing*. His most famous work deals with gynaecology.

We get an insight into the prescriptions made by the healing **shrines of Aesclepius** at Pergamum from the accounts of Aelius Aristides (AD 117–87), a teacher of rhetoric. Aristides suffered from a variety of ailments including asthma and dropsy. When he had a high fever he was urged to bathe several times in an ice-cold river, and to run a mile at full speed. At other times he was covered in blankets, dipped in warm baths, and bled. Blood-letting in ancient times may have killed as many patients as diseases.

Roman towns

Roman buildings

The Romans invented concrete, making it out of two parts of a volcanic ash called *pozzolana* (after the town of Puteoli) mixed with one part of lime. With this light-weight concrete the Romans made brilliant use of the arch, the vault and the dome in their buildings. Agrippa's Pantheon in Rome, rebuilt by the Emperor Hadrian, is one of the most impressive domes ever built, and is almost 150 feet (45 m) in diameter. The Emperor Domitian's palace used barrel-vaults 100 feet (30 m) across.

But despite their architectural abilities, very few Romans could afford a separate house. In Rome there were twenty-six blocks of flats or apartments for every individual house. Luxurious villas preserved at Pompeii and Herculaneum contrast with the remains of flats at the Roman port of Ostia.

Profiteering landlords, such as the politician Crassus, built taller and taller blocks of flats until the Emperor Augustus limited their height to 70 feet (21 metres), or about six storeys. Unlike modern blocks of flats with penthouses on the top floors, the most expensive flats were located on the ground floor, unless they were taken up by shops (*tabernae*). The higher the flat, the cheaper, more squalid and more crowded it became. Rents ranged from 30,000 denarii per year on the ground floor to 2,000 denarii for upstairs flats.

One of the greatest problems for people occupying the highest flats was the labour involved in carrying up water. Because of the flimsy building materials sometimes used, many apartments were firetraps. As the poet Juvenal wrote:

> Who, on Tivoli's heights, or a
>   small town like Gabii, say,
> Fears the collapse of his
>   house? But Rome is
>   supported on pipestems,
> Matchsticks; it's cheaper, so,
>   for the landlord to shore up
>   his ruins,
> Patch up the old cracked walls,
>   and notify all the tenants
> They can sleep secure, though
>   the beams are in ruins
>   above them.
> No, the place to live is out
>   there, where none cry *Fire*!
> Sounds the alarm of the night,
>   with a neighbour yelling for
>   water,
> Moving his chattels and goods,
>   and the whole third floor is
>   smoking.

The frequent fires were more than a match for the 3,000 *vigiles*, a corps of freedmen who Augustus had set up as fire-fighters and policemen. The fire which devastated Rome during Nero's reign in AD 64 was simply the worst in a long series.

Next page: an artist's impression of a typical Roman town centre *(forum)*. Beside the temple stands a row of shops. In the foreground is the public fountain. Local farmers and merchants have set up stalls in the middle of the forum to sell their goods.

A model of Rome as it probably looked in the fourth century AD. On the left is the Circus Maximus which held 250,000 spectators.

Aqueducts

Among the greatest examples of the skill of Roman engineers were the marvellous aqueducts which they built both in Rome and elsewhere. The first aqueduct for Rome was built in 312 BC. Major aqueducts were built by Agrippa under the Emperor Augustus, and by the Emperor Claudius. It has been estimated that these supplied the city of Rome with between 200 and 300 million gallons (910–1360 million litres) of water per day. With justifiable pride, Frontinus, the controller of water supplies, declared: 'Will anybody compare the idle pyramids or those other useless though renowned works of the Greeks with these aqueducts, these many indispensable structures.'

At Caesarea, in Palestine, archaeologists have uncovered the remains of both a high-level and a low-level aqueduct. These brought water from about 5 miles away on a system of arches over marshy areas. The three-tiered Pont du Gard in Nimes, France, carries water across a river valley. The two-storey aqueduct in Segovia, Spain, built by Augustus as part of a 60-mile (96 km) water supply system, is still in use today.

Roman aqueducts consisted of a cement-lined rectangular pipe supported on arches. The photograph shows the Pont du Gard aqueduct in France.

Refuse disposal

When the apostle Paul compared his past achievements to the glory of knowing Christ, he described them with a word meaning 'something thrown to the dogs'. He probably had in mind rubbish which was frequently thrown out into the streets for scavenging dogs. At times refuse was hurled out of upper-storey windows, as Juvenal warned:

> Look at other things, the various dangers of night-time.
> How high it is to the cornice that breaks, and a chunk beats my brains out,
> Or some slob heaves a jar, broken or cracked, from a window.
> There are as many deaths in the night as there are open windows
> Where you pass by; if you're wise, you will pray, in your wretched devotions,
> People may be content with no

The remains of the Roman public lavatories at Ostia in Italy.

more than emptying slop jars.

Dwellers in the upper storeys were supposed to dispose of the sewage from chamber pots in cess trenches. But they often emptied the contents of these jars out of the windows, to the peril of the unwary passer-by! Public urinals were placed in front of laundry shops, since urine was used in cleaning clothes, and public latrines could be used for a nominal fee. The latrines were flushed with water from the aqueducts and emptied into the vast system of underground sewers. The greatest of these, the *Cloaca Maxima*, emptied into the Tiber.

The baths

The most important amenity which Romans could enjoy, poor and wealthy alike, was the comfort of the public baths. At first the baths charged a modest fee, but later they became free. In the period of Augustus there were 170 baths in Rome, and they became so popular that before the end of the first century AD there were nearly 1,000, most of them small establishments.

The emperors established truly extravagant baths; Nero's contained 1,600 marble bath seats. The largest of all were the 33 acre Baths of Caracalla and the 32 acre baths of Diocletian, both built in the third century AD.

The baths themselves consisted of various specialized rooms: the dressing room (*apodyterium*), the rubbing room (*unctorium*), the steam room (*laconicum*), the hot bath (*caldarium*), warm bath (*tepidarium*), and the cold bath (*frigidarium*). The imperial *thermae*, however, were more than baths; they were miniature cities. They included rooms for wrestling and exercise, libraries, museums, gardens, shops, restaurants, gaming-rooms

The Baths of Caracalla, once a recreation centre for the people of Rome.

and brothels. The baths opened at noon and closed at sunset. Men and women bathed together, until the reign of Hadrian, when women came during the early hours and men later. The baths teemed with humanity and were extremely noisy. The writer Seneca, who once lived over a public bath, described the scene:

> When your strenuous gentleman, for example, is exercising himself by flourishing lead-weights; when he is working hard or else pretending to work hard, I can hear him grunt, and when he releases his imprisoned breath, I can hear him panting in wheezy and high-pitched tones. . . . Add to this the arrest of an occasional roisterer or pickpocket, the racket of the man who always likes to hear his own voice in the bathroom, or the enthusiast who plunges into the swimming tank with unconscionable noise and splashing.'

Baths were considered such indispensable features of civilized life that King Herod the Great had *thermae* built at Herodium, Machaerus and Masada in Palestine – all places where water was in short supply.

Roman roads

The streets of Rome were generally narrow, between 13 and 16 feet (4 and 5 metres) wide. Stepping stones were sometimes placed at crossroads, and can still be seen at Pompeii.

Because of increasing traffic problems in Rome, Julius Caesar banned all vehicles between sunrise and four p.m. with four exceptions: wagons for construction or demolition; triumphal chariots; funeral processions; and the carriages of the drowsiest son of a sea-cow.

One of the most impressive achievements of the Romans was the vast network of roads which they built to hold together their far-flung Empire. The major roads were begun as early as the third century BC but they were most extensively developed in the early years of the Empire. Ultimately the Romans constructed 250,000 miles of paved roads, many of them new

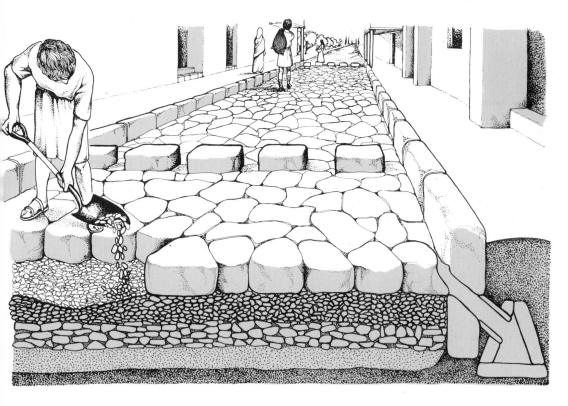

A Roman road being constructed. A level base was made with sand or lime mortar. Layers of broken stones and gravel were laid over it, and blocks of stone set in concrete formed the hard top surface. Drainage channels carried rainwater away. Stepping stones slowed down the traffic in towns and enabled pedestrians to keep dry as they crossed the road.

The baths were magnificent buildings decorated with marble and gold. This is an artist's impression of bathers in the *tepidarium* (warm room) of the Baths of Diocletian, now part of the church of S. Maria degli Angeli.

the vestal virgins and priests. This meant that most goods waggons creaked into the city in the evening or at night, making it difficult for city dwellers to get any sleep. Juvenal complained:

Who but the rich can afford
    sleep and a garden flat?
That's the source of infection.
    The wheels creak by on the
    narrow
Streets of the districts, the
    drivers squabble and brawl
    when they're stopped,
More than enough to frustrate

routes, which went as straight as an arrow.

When constructing a road, the engineers dug a foundation trench about 3 feet (1 m) deep. They then laid a foundation of sand, stones, gravel and concrete, on top of which they laid cobble-stones in mortar. In towns the cobbles would be flat slabs; elsewhere they would be irregular stones.

The Romans built splendid river-bridges, some of which still stand, such as the Ponte Grosso

A stretch of the Egnatian Way, the Roman road running across the north of Greece linking the Adriatic coast with the Bosphorus. This picture was taken near Philippi.

garrisons at intervals along the route'.

Five principal roads radiated from Rome, including the famous Appian Way (*Via Appia*) built by Appius Claudius in 321 BC, from Rome to Capua. At Capua, near Neapolis (Naples), the road branched in two: one trunk went to Messina at the toe of Italy, and the other to Brundisium at the heel of Italy. The Appian Way was unusually wide, between 14 and 20 feet across (4–6 metres), with room for two carriages to pass side by side.

The Egnatian Way (*Via Egnatia*) went from Dyrrhachium on the west coast of Macedonia to Thessalonica, Amphipolis, Philippi and finally to Constantinople, a total distance of about 500 miles/800 kilometres. This was the route that Paul, Silas and Timothy took on their travels.

Though some of the roads in Palestine may have been constructed as early as the time of the Emperor Augustus, most of the 50,000 paved roads in Palestine and Syria were constructed under Trajan and Hadrian. The famous 'Street called Straight' (*Via Recta*) in Damascus, where Paul stayed (Acts 9:11), is today called the Bab Sharqi Street. It is still marked by a Roman arch, which the Syrians recently found about 13 feet/4 metres below the present street level, and a triple arch at the eastern end of the street.

The network of Roman roads was constructed primarily to permit the easy movement of troops, and also to serve the imperial postal service begun by Augustus. The Roman copy of the Persian 'pony express' was provided with changes of horses every 10 miles/16 kilometres and with 'inns' at 25-mile/40-kilometre intervals. The couriers could average 120 miles/192 kilometres per day.

Inns for the general public were also available. Christians from Rome met Paul after his

on the Via Flaminia from Rome to Rimini in north Italy. The well-preserved bridge over the River Tagus in Lusitania (Portugal) is 617 feet (188 m) long, and its arches nearly 90 feet (27 m) in diameter. It was paid for by eleven leading local citizens.

Roads were measured from the golden milestone in the forum in Rome itself. The Roman mile measured a thousand paces, from the Latin for one thousand (*mille*). It was slightly shorter than the English mile, 1,620 yards (1,480 metres) as opposed to 1,760 yards (1,608 metres). Stone posts between 6 and 8 feet tall (1·8–2·4 metres) were erected to mark each mile. During the Republic these stones simply marked distances, but during the Empire they also recorded the name of the emperor. A mile post in Yugoslavia records that Trajan 'built this road by cutting through mountains and eliminating the curves.' In Egypt a mile-stone built when Hadrian was emperor informs us that he supplied the road 'with plentiful cisterns, resting stations and arrival in Italy at a place called The Three Taverns, 43 miles/69 kilometres from Rome (Acts 28:15). Often these establishments had unsavoury reputations because of dishonest innkeepers, crowds of brigands and bug-infested rooms. The well-to-do, who travelled with large retinues, preferred to set up their own tents where the climate allowed it. A network of friends who were willing to offer accommodation made travel much easier.

The average rate of travel for pedestrians was 3 miles/4·8 kilometres per hour. Soldiers were expected to march 4 miles/ 6·4 kilometres per hour, and on forced marches 5 miles/8 kilometres per hour. The average distance covered in a day on foot would be between 15 and 20 miles (24–32 kilometres); 20 miles for donkey caravans; and from 25 to 50 miles (40–80 kilometres) for carriages. Julius Caesar once covered the

800 miles/1,240 kilometres from the River Rhone to Rome in eight days. Tiberius set the record by covering 200 miles/320 kilometres in twenty-five hours.

The superb Roman road network was made use of by Christian missionaries such as Paul for the spreading of the Christian good news. Irenaeus of France wrote in about AD 180: 'The Romans have given the world peace and we travel without fear along the roads and across the sea wherever we will.'

Christians practised hospitality and built up a worldwide community which helped travellers. The *Didache*, an early Christian writing, warned against the abuse of Christian hospitality: 'Let every apostle, when he comes to you, be received as the Lord; but he shall not stay more than a single day, or, if necessary, a second day; but if he stays three days, he is a false prophet.'

Roman roads.

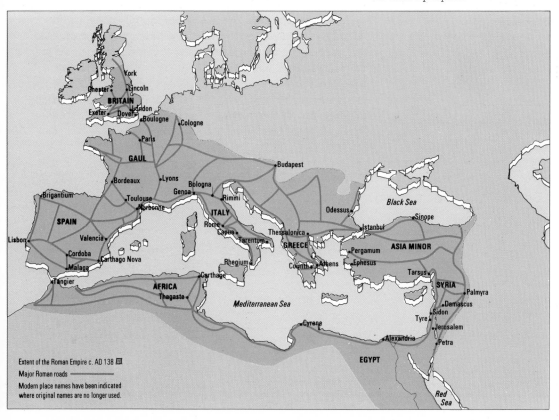

Extent of the Roman Empire c. AD 138 ▦

Major Roman roads ———

Modern place names have been indicated where original names are no longer used.

Sports and pastimes

Roman drama   The Romans developed their drama relatively late in the Republic, and consciously imitated that of the Greeks. Roman tragedies were never popular, and those written by Seneca were designed for recitation rather than for performance. Plautus (254–184 BC) and Terence (195–159 BC) were the most successful writers of Roman comedy. They adapted freely from Menander, the Hellenistic writer of New Comedy. The Romans were quite prepared to laugh at the weaknesses of the Greeks.

Wooden theatres were built as early as 179 BC. The first stone theatre was built for Pompey in 55 BC, and could seat 28,000. The theatre of Balbus, built in Rome in 13 BC, could hold 8,000. The theatre of Marcellus, which was built in AD 11 and held 15,000 seats, is still standing and has been converted into flats. One historian points out that the 'theatre was, in fact, too big for the play.' Plots were made simple for the very large, unsophisticated audiences.

Actors and actresses were easily identified by their costumes: white for old men, purple for the rich, and yellow for prostitutes. The reputations of actresses were so notorious, in fact, that they were classed with prostitutes. Ballets and pantomimes were popular. The Romans enjoyed mime which professed to be a 'slice of life'. In them actresses took off their clothes, sexual intercourse was performed, criminals were tortured and sometimes crucified on stage.

The theatre at Ephesus seated about 25,000 spectators.

The races Chariot races were the source of the greatest excitement in Rome, and were held in the Circus Maximus below the Palatine Hill. This great hippodrome, which still stands, is 215 yards/200 metres wide and 645 yards/600 metres long. By the period of the Flavian emperors it could seat 255,000 spectators.

The chariots, which were ordinarily pulled by four horses, ran around the central island seven times – a distance of about 2 miles/3 kilometres. The charioteers' skill lay in making the hazardous counter-clockwise turns as closely as possible. Much of the excitement, as in modern motor racing, lay in the element of danger. The crowds expected to see some spectacular crashes, or a driver dragged to his death.

The races were among the most popular subjects of daily conversation. The historian Tacitus exclaimed: 'Few people can be found who talk of any other subjects in their homes; and whenever we enter a classroom, what else is the conversation

Chariot racing was a popular but dangerous sport.

of the youths?' Teachers complained that their pupils could not concentrate on their lessons on the days of the races as the roar of the great crowd in the Circus Maximus could be heard all over the city. Little boys played in toy chariots pulled by goats and dogs.

The chariots and their drivers were sponsored by four corporations known as the Whites, Greens, Blues and Reds. The lower class charioteers became popular and wealthy if they won. The writer Juvenal declared, 'A hundred lawyers hardly make as much as that Red race-driver, "The Lizard".' Diocles, a driver for the Reds about AD 150, won over 2,000 races and amassed over thirty-five million sesterces (over one million pounds).

Gambling on races bordered on the fanatical. When Poppaea criticized her husband Nero's addiction to the races, he kicked his pregnant wife in the stomach and caused her death. Like the fans at soccer matches, supporters of rival factions often rioted. The most spectacular of these was the infamous Nika riot, which took place in the hippodrome at Constantinople in AD 532. The supporters of the Greens and the Blues fought each other, and some 30,000 people were killed. Chariot races were finally forbidden in AD 549.

Gladiators and the games

Among the worst aspects of Roman culture were the bloody gladiatorial games, which became increasingly popular over the centuries.

The games were originated by the early inhabitants of Rome, the Etruscans, who sacrificed prisoners of war to the spirits of their own fallen warriors. During the Roman Republic it became customary for the 'mayors' to sponsor such games out of their own funds to curry favour with the public. Julius Caesar made a great impression by sponsoring fights between 320 pairs of gladiators in 65 BC.

The Emperor Augustus sponsored twenty-seven shows in which a total of 10,000 fighters appeared, and twenty-six contests involving African animals in which 3,500 beasts were killed. When the Emperor Titus dedicated the Flavian Amphitheatre in AD 80, he held 100 days of games in which he used 2,500 captives from Judea. Trajan celebrated his Dacian conquests by holding four months of games involving 5,000 pairs of gladiators.

A cross-section of the Colosseum, originally known as the Flavian Amphitheatre. It could hold about 50,000 spectators who were shielded from the sun by a canopy. The central arena was about 80 metres by 50 metres. The amphitheatre was equipped with subterranean cages for animals and mechanical lifts to bring them to the main floor. It could be flooded for naval battles.

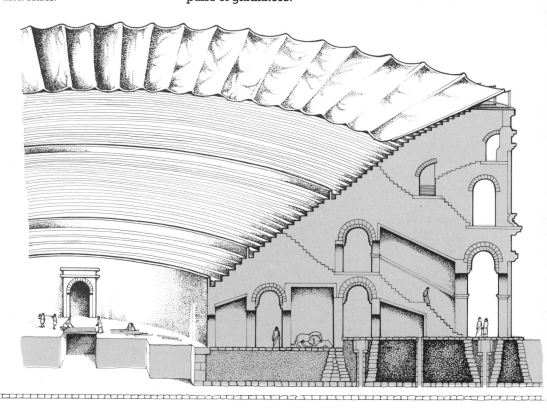

In Caesar's time there were 132 holidays each year. By the reign of Claudius the number had risen to 159, ninety-three of them devoted to gladiatorial games. By the third century AD there were 200 holidays, and 175 of these were devoted to games; there were by then more holidays than working days in a year.

The games included the hunting or combats of wild beasts. In providing beasts for these spectacles, entire species, such as the hippos of Nubia, the elephants of north Africa, and the lions of Mesopotamia, were exterminated. The Romans sought even more bizarre animals; Caesar introduced the giraffe, tigers were imported from Parthia, rhinos and crocodiles were also introduced. The orator Cicero was appalled: 'What pleasure can a cultivated man take in seeing a huge animal tear a weak man to pieces, or a splendid animal pierced by a spear?'

The humans who were forced to fight were usually criminals or prisoners of war. But there were also professional gladiators who were trained in schools at Rome, Capua and Pompeii. Juvenal expressed his disgust at the 'women's liberation' movement of his day, which went so far as to promote women gladiators.

Gladiators known as Samnites fought in heavy armour, while others, known as the Retiari, were armed only with a net, a trident and a dagger. The combatants would appear before the emperor and cry out: 'Hail, emperor, those who are about to die salute you.' When a man fell, the crowd could either plead for his life or scream for his death. If they wished to spare him they would wave their handkerchiefs, hold their thumbs up, and cry 'Mitte'. If they wished him killed, they would point their thumbs down, and shout 'Iugula', and the victim would be stabbed in the throat. The bodies were then removed and the sand would be raked over, so that fresh combatants could appear.

Champion gladiators depicted on a fourth-century AD Roman mosaic.

Gladiators literally fought for their lives. This drawing is of a Retarius with his net and trident confronting a Samnite armed with a sword and shield.

There were relatively few protests voiced against the brutality of the games. Cicero simply commented, 'This type of display is apt to seem cruel and brutal to some eyes, and I incline to think that it is so, as now conducted.' Seneca objected to the senseless killing which continued even during intermissions: 'The conclusion of every fight is death; no quarter is given. And this goes on (even) while the stands are empty. "But the fellow was a highwayman; he killed a man!" So what? Because he killed a man he deserves this fate, but what did you do, poor man, to deserve having to watch?' Only a few emperors, such as Tiberius and Marcus Aurelius, disliked the games. Marcus Aurelius' unworthy son, Commodus, enjoyed taking part in such games himself.

Jewish rabbis objected to the games because of the idolatry associated with them. Rabbi Meir said, 'It is forbidden to go to the amphitheatres of the gentiles because of idolatry.' A Jewish writing on 'Idolatrous Worship' stated: 'A person is permitted to go to the gentiles' amphitheatre if he is taking part in public business. However, if he is a prominent figure in the Jewish community, it is forbidden. A person who sits in the stadium is guilty of bloodshed. Rabbi Nathan permits it because, as a spectator, he may shout for mercy and thus save lives; and he may be able to testify (that a woman's husband has been killed)

Wild animals were hunted and transported to Rome for the games. This third or fourth-century AD mosaic from Sicily shows a tigress being captured.

so as to enable a woman to remarry.'

From the time of the great fire in Nero's Rome in AD 64, Christians provided many of the victims for the games. The historian Tacitus described Nero's cruelty: 'Mockery of every sort was added to their deaths. Covered with the skins of beasts, they were torn by dogs and perished, or were nailed to crosses, or were doomed to the flames and burnt, to serve as a nightly illumination when daylight had gone.' Later Christians were made scapegoats for other disasters, such as plagues and famines. In those times, according to the Christian writer Tertullian, the cry was: 'The Christians to the lion!'

Gladiatorial games were finally stopped in AD 404 by the Emperor Honorius, when a monk was killed as he tried to separate the fighters in an arena. But games using animals continued until AD 681.

Roman religion

The Roman gods

Roman religion originated in religion of the soil, which reverenced a mysterious, impersonal force (*numen*) which pervaded nature. The Romans placed a strong emphasis on the right rituals. The word 'religion' comes from a Latin word meaning 'to bind'; religion was a contract summed up in a Latin phrase meaning 'I give in order that you may give.'

The Romans were concerned to maintain the 'peace of the gods' by such means as sin offerings and a banquet featuring the images of the gods. Every Roman made offerings at each meal to the spirits of the farm and the larder. In the period of the Republic, the Romans took over many Greek myths and identified the gods of the Greeks with their own native gods.

Jupiter (the Greek Zeus) was 'the best and the greatest'. His temple was built on the Capitoline Hill in Rome, copying Etruscan models, and was the most important of all. He was believed to make known his will through lightning and thunder. It was to Jupiter's temple that a victorious general or emperor made his way in the 'triumph', a ceremonial procession in which prisoners and booty were paraded.

Juno (the Greek Hera) presided over women and marriage. Her month, the second half of June, was a period considered propitious for marriages. Her temple on the Capitoline Hill, known as *Moneta*, 'the Warner', served to mint coins, and has given us the word 'money'.

Mars (the Greek Ares), the god of war, was second in importance only to Jupiter. His priests, the Salii, danced in full armour on the Campus Martius or 'Field of Mars' in the month named after him, March.

Vesta (the Greek Hestia), the goddess of the state hearth, was attended by six vestal virgins who each served her for

The most popular Roman festival was Saturnalia, held in mid-December in honour of Saturn, the god of agriculture. Everyone, including slaves, joined in. This modern sculpture has captured the abandoned mood of the festival.

Top: Mercury, protector of flocks, thieves and merchants.

Above: Mars, the god of war.

Below: Jupiter, the chief Roman god.

thirty years. Any vestal virgin who was found to be unchaste was buried alive. The virgins had to keep a perpetual flame burning on her altar; it was not finally extinguished until AD 382.

Neptune (the Greek Poseidon) was the god not only of the sea but of rivers. His priests were known as *pontifices*, literally 'bridge builders'. Their leader, the *pontifex maximus*, was an elected official who supervised the religious calendar and sacrifices. The title has survived and is today applied to the 'supreme pontiff' or pope, of the Roman Catholic Church.

Mercury (the Greek Hermes) was the god of both merchants and thieves – an intriguing combination. His temple was located on the Aventine Hill in Rome. Venus (the Greek Aphrodite) was the god of love and beauty. An important cult to her was imported in 217 BC during the Second Punic War from the Phoenician colony of Eryx, in western Sicily, where sacred prostitution was practised. In Corinth a thousand sacred prostitutes of her cult plied their trade, but the Romans did not encourage the practice.

Many of the months of our year are named after words from Roman religion: January is named after the two-faced god Janus, whose gate was kept open during times of war and shut in times of peace. It was usually open! February is named after *februa*, the rites used in the primitive fertility ceremony of the Lupercalia. Thongs made from the hides of sacrificed goats and dogs were believed to give fertility to barren women. April is the month for the earth to open (*aperire* in Latin). May comes from *maius* 'greater', a title of Jupiter. July was named after Julius Caesar and August after Augustus. October, November and December were originally the eighth, ninth and tenth months of the year (their meaning in Latin) as the Roman year originally began in March.

Divination

The prediction of future events and the interpretation of past occurrences (divination) played a major role in Roman religion and in politics and military activities too.

The Romans regarded unusual occurrences as signs that the peace of the gods had been broken. Prodigies they noted included such freaks as a foal with five feet, hot stones falling from heaven, or shields sweating blood.

The Romans were especially concerned to discover the will of the gods from observing the signs given by birds (*auspices*). From the temple precinct they would watch the flight of birds, their numbers, and their sounds. The Romans also observed the feeding of chickens on their military campaigns. When some of his sacred chickens did not eat, an impatient naval commander threw them into the sea with the remark, 'Let them drink since they will not eat!' – an impious act which was said to have cost him the battle.

No military campaign or official act was supposed to be

conducted without discovering the will of the gods by some act of divination. To disregard the signs or ignore the stars spelt disaster. Julius Caesar was forewarned of his assassination by dreams and other omens which he ignored.

From their Etruscan predecessors the Romans learned to interpret various kinds of lightning and thunder. From the Etruscans too the Romans learned the art of divination by the examination of the intestines of animal sacrifices. A diviner was attached to the various army units.

Such practices of divination continued until the end of the Empire. It was Christians making the sign of the cross to counteract the sacrifices of pagan soothsayers that enraged the Emperor Diocletian and his Caesar Galienus in AD 298 and resulted in a savage persecution of Christians. Even the Emperor Constantine, who between AD 318 and 320 passed laws to forbid black magic and to prevent soothsayers from entering private houses, permitted divination to find out what it meant if lightning struck a public building.

These model hands are marked with magic signs to ward off evil.

Emperor worship

The pharaohs of ancient Egypt were long considered to be divine. Alexander the Great demanded that people prostrate themselves before him, and his successor in Egypt, Ptolemy, continued the cult of the divine king. Roman generals in the east had been given divine honours by Greek cities as early as the second century BC. Julius Caesar was declared divine by the Senate in 42 BC, two years after his assassination, and this act laid the foundation for the cult of emperor worship.

Though the Emperor Augustus accepted divine honours from the east, he discouraged such tributes in the west. A drink offering was poured to his guardian spirit at every public and private banquet. King Herod the Great built temples to Augustus both at Caesarea and at Sebaste. The poets Virgil and Horace praised Augustus with extravagant homage. But when Agrippa built the Pantheon in Rome in 25 BC Augustus declined to have it dedicated as a temple to himself. Only when he died was he raised to the status of a god by the Senate.

The Emperor Tiberius forbade the deification of his mother, the Empress Livia. As an evil emperor, he was himself deprived of this honour by the Senate. And Gaius Caligula, the crazed emperor, not only demanded divine honours for himself, but he even had his sister Drusilla deified after her death. The Senate took revenge after he died by blackening his memory.

Claudius refused divine honours, though he did accept a temple dedicated to him as a sign of political loyalty in the recently conquered province of Britain. But the vain emperor Nero had a colossal statue of himself erected with his face as the sun-god, Apollo Helios. He declined to have a temple of the god Nero erected in Rome, however, commenting that 'the princeps does not receive the honour of a god until he has ceased to be among men'. After his death the Senate denied him this honour.

Vespasian, who was regarded as a good emperor, joked as he was dying, 'Dear me! I must be turning into a god!' His popular son Titus, whose brief reign was cut short by illness, was presented with a cult after his death by his brother Domitian. Domitian himself, who demanded that people address him as 'Lord and God', persecuted Jews and Christians who refused to regard him as divine. Universally feared and disliked during his life, Domitian was condemned by everyone after his death.

Emperors had been regarded as specially favoured by the gods even before some claimed to be divine. This cameo shows the Emperor Augustus, seated beside the goddess Roma, being crowned by Cybele who is attended by Neptune and Fortune. It was made to commemorate the victory of Tiberius (who stands in front of the chariot) over the Pannonians.

Christians were quite willing to pray for the emperor and to obey the Roman authorities. In a letter to Timothy Paul urged

1 Timothy 2:1-3

'that petitions, prayers, requests and thanksgivings be offered to God for all people, for kings and all others in authority.' He also wrote to Christians in Rome that 'Everyone must obey the

Romans 13: 1

state authorities, because no authority exists without God's permission, and the existing authorities have been put there by God.' But the Christians were not willing to offer sacrifices to the emperor's cult. Jews also held this position, but were tolerated as a national 'recognized religion'. Christians, who were made up of many nationalities, were suspected of being an immoral secret society. When they refused to sacrifice they were considered guilty of treason and were persecuted accordingly.

The emperor cult was mainly of political importance rather

than religious. There is no evidence of prayers to the deified emperors. In all the Roman provinces the official imperial cult was organized by civic magistrates to foster loyalty to Rome. Roman religion was above all a cult of the state. One historian has emphasized that 'the worship of the Roman gods was a civic duty, the worship of foreign gods the expression of personal belief'. In the later years of the Republic and during the Empire many Romans turned increasingly to the so-called 'oriental mystery religions' from the Near East.

Jews and Christians

According to the Roman historian Suetonius, the Emperor Claudius (AD 41–54) expelled from Rome Jews who were apparently causing disturbances 'at the instigation of Chrestus'. Chrestus may be a variant name for Jesus Christ, and the agitation may have been brought about by Jewish-Christian teachers such as Aquila and Priscilla. They were forced to leave Rome in AD 49 and met Paul two years later at Corinth. As the writer Dio Cassius reported that Claudius simply forbade the Jews from holding their meetings, the expulsion was probably not total in its effect. Nor is there any record of Jewish-Christian clashes in Paul's letter to the Romans.

Acts 18: 1-2

Certainly Paul's letter indicates that there was a sizeable group of Christians in the city before AD 60, and his letter names five household churches. By tradition both he and Peter were martyred in the city, although the evidence is not conclusive.

Nero's wife Poppaea may have been a Jewish convert, and was certainly sympathetic to the Jews. When the historian Josephus came to Rome in AD 64 he was introduced to Poppaea by a Jewish actor, a favourite of Nero. It was in Nero's reign that the great revolt of the Jews broke out in Palestine in 66. Nero began work on a canal planned to cross the Corinthian Isthmus, while he was staying in Greece, and he used Jewish prisoners as labourers who had been sent to him by the general Vespasian.

The end of the war against the Jews brought thousands of Jewish prisoners to Rome to march in the triumphal procession of Titus, and to perform in the gladiatorial games. Titus was accompanied by his mistress, the Herodian princess, Berenice. Under the Flavian emperors Josephus was made a Roman citizen, given a pension, and the Roman name of Flavius.

The Emperor Domitian persecuted both Jews and Christians. Among those he condemned to death was his own cousin Flavius Clemens, who was charged with 'atheism' and 'Jewish customs'. Clemens' wife, Domitilla, who was exiled, was claimed to be a Christian by the church historian Eusebius. Much later traditions claimed that Clemens himself was also a Christian.

Christians in Rome were frequently persecuted from the first to the fourth century AD. Their art reflects their beliefs. This painting of Jesus as the good shepherd is from a second-century Christian catacomb in Rome.

Archaeologists have found evidence about the Jews in Rome chiefly in their catacombs. The Jews, who were accustomed to carve out funeral chambers in the limestone of Palestine, transferred this custom to the soft, volcanic tufa-stone of Rome. Three large Jewish catacombs survive: the oldest in Monteverde may have been used as early as the first century BC; those on the Via Appia and the Via Nomentana were in use from the first to the third centuries AD.

It is significant that 76 per cent of the catacomb inscriptions are in Greek, 23 per cent in Latin, and only 1 per cent in Hebrew or Aramaic. They reveal that many of the Roman Jews were poor, only a few were wealthy. The inscriptions also reveal that seven out of the eleven synagogues in Rome were located outside the main city, across the River Tiber, in a generally squalid and crowded area.

In 1961 a synagogue was discovered at Ostia, the port at the mouth of the River Tiber. Part of the building was begun at the end of the first century AD. Graffiti discovered at Pompeii show that Jews lived there before its destruction in AD 79. One of the Jews, or possibly a Christian, described the decadent immorality of the city by writing on the wall, 'Sodom and Gomorrah'.

Jews feature prominently in Roman satirical literature as objects of scorn. The poet Horace alluded to their seeking converts and their faith in miracles. The writers Seneca and Juvenal objected to the idleness of the Jews on the sabbath. Petronius was puzzled at their abstinence from pork. The historian Tacitus repeated scurrilous anti-Semitic explanations of their dietary scruples.